ARCHITECT REGISTRATION EXAM

STRUCTURAL SYSTEMS

ARE SAMPLE PROBLEMS AND PRACTICE EXAM

RIMA TAHER, PhD

The Power to Pass™
www.ppi2pass.com

Professional Publications, Inc. • Belmont, California

Benefit by Registering this Book with PPI

- Get book updates and corrections
- Hear the latest exam news
- Obtain exclusive exam tips and strategies
- Receive special discounts

Register your book at **www.ppi2pass.com/register**.

Report Errors and View Corrections for this Book

PPI is grateful to every reader who notifies us of a possible error. Your feedback allows us to improve the quality and accuracy of our products. You can report errata and view corrections at **www.ppi2pass.com/errata**.

STRUCTURAL SYSTEMS: ARE SAMPLE PROBLEMS AND PRACTICE EXAM

Current printing of this edition: 3

Printing History

edition number	printing number	update
1	1	New book.
1	2	Minor corrections.
1	3	Minor corrections.

Printed in the United States of America

PPI
1250 Fifth Avenue, Belmont, CA 94002
(650) 593-9119
www.ppi2pass.com

ISBN: 978-1-59126-127-8

TABLE OF CONTENTS

PREFACE AND ACKNOWLEDGMENTS

This book is tailored to the needs of those studying for version 4.0 of the Architect Registration Examination. The ARE 4.0 is one step in a process of change that began in 2001, when the National Council of Architectural Registration Boards (NCARB) published the results of a two-year study of the architecture profession. Since then, in response to that study, NCARB has introduced a series of changes to the ARE. Previous versions of the ARE have reduced the number of graphic vignettes and introduced new types of questions. Version 4.0, though, is the most substantial change yet, reorganizing and reducing the number of divisions and integrating graphic vignettes into divisions that were previously multiple choice only.

In the ARE 4.0, NCARB has eliminated the graphics-only Building Technology division and redistributed its six graphic vignettes into other divisions, combining them with multiple-choice sections of the exam. Each multiple-choice section carried over from version 3.1 now contains fewer questions, and a multiple-choice section has been added to the Site Planning & Design division (formerly called just Site Planning). The two structural divisions from version 3.1, General Structures and Lateral Forces, are now combined into one division, Structural Systems. In all, there are now seven divisions instead of nine, and there are somewhat fewer multiple-choice questions in all on the ARE 4.0 than on version 3.1.

In response to the version 4.0 changes, PPI has reorganized and revised its ARE review books. *ARE Review Manual* now covers all the divisions of the ARE in a single volume. This new book, *Structural Systems: ARE Sample Problems and Practice Exam*, is one of seven companion volumes, one for each ARE 4.0 division. We believe that this organization will help you study for individual divisions most effectively.

You will find that this book and the related volumes are valuable parts of your exam preparation. Although there is no substitute for a good formal education and the broad-based experience provided by your internship with a practicing architect, this review series will help direct your study efforts to increase your chances of passing the ARE.

Many people have helped in the production of this book. I would like to thank all the fine people at PPI including Scott Marley (project editor), Courtnee Crystal (editorial assistant), Amy Schwertman (typesetter, cover designer, and illustrator), and Thomas Bergstrom (illustrator).

Rima Taher, PhD

ABOUT THE AUTHOR

Rima Taher has many years of experience teaching structures classes for architecture students. She is a special lecturer at the New Jersey School of Architecture, New Jersey Institute of Technology (NJIT), where she has taught structures courses to both undergraduate and graduate students since 1989. She has also taught review courses for the Architect Registration Examination (ARE) in general structures and lateral forces since 2002. She received a university-wide award of teaching excellence from NJIT in 1999.

In 1982, Dr. Taher earned her bachelor of civil engineering degree from the Institut National des Sciences Appliquées de Lyon. She earned her master of civil engineering degree in 1983 from the historic and prestigious École Nationale des Ponts et Chaussées in Paris, where in 1986 she also earned her doctorate in civil engineering with high honors, with a specialty in building science and technology.

An active member of the American Society of Civil Engineers (ASCE), Dr. Taher serves on the structural technical committee of ASCE at the North Jersey branch. She has practiced civil, geotechnical, and structural engineering for several years at well-known engineering firms in New Jersey, including Clinton Bogert Associates and Converse Consultants. She still practices structural engineering part-time through local firms.

Dr. Taher has participated in research work in building technology, including research into wind engineering and structural design for high winds and hurricanes. She has lectured at the Wind Engineering Research Center at Tokyo Polytechnic University and has published articles on wind engineering in conference proceedings and in civil engineering publications and journals.

Dr. Taher lives with her teenage daughter in Clifton, New Jersey. She likes to travel and enjoys swimming, playing tennis, and reading.

INTRODUCTION

ABOUT THIS BOOK

Structural Systems: ARE Sample Problems and Practice Exam is written to help you prepare for the Structural Systems division of the Architect Registration Examination (ARE), version 4.0.

Although this book can be a valuable study aid by itself, it is designed to be used along with the *ARE Review Manual*, also published by PPI. The *ARE Review Manual* is organized into sections that cover all seven divisions of the ARE 4.0.

- Programming, Planning & Practice
- Site Planning & Design
- Schematic Design
- Structural Systems
- Building Systems
- Building Design & Construction Systems
- Construction Documents & Services

This book is one of seven companion volumes to the *ARE Review Manual* that PPI publishes. Each of these books contains sample problems and practice exams for one of the ARE 4.0 divisions.

- *Programming, Planning & Practice: ARE Sample Problems and Practice Exam*
- *Site Planning & Design: ARE Sample Problems and Practice Exam*
- *Schematic Design: ARE Sample Problems and Practice Exam*
- *Structural Systems: ARE Sample Problems and Practice Exam*
- *Building Systems: ARE Sample Problems and Practice Exam*
- *Building Design & Construction Systems: ARE Sample Problems and Practice Exam*
- *Construction Documents & Services: ARE Sample Problems and Practice Exam*

THE ARCHITECT REGISTRATION EXAMINATION

Congratulations on completing (or nearing the end of) the Intern Development Program! You are two-thirds of the way to being able to call yourself an architect. NAAB degree? Check. IDP? Check. Now on to step three.

The final hurdle is the Architect Registration Examination. The ARE is a uniform test administered to candidates who wish to become licensed architects after they have served their required internships. It is given in all fifty states, all ten Canadian provinces, and five other jurisdictions including the District of Columbia, Guam, the Northern Mariana Islands, Puerto Rico, and the Virgin Islands.

The ARE has been developed to protect the health, safety, and welfare of the public by testing a candidate's entry-level competence to practice architecture. Its content relates as closely as possible to situations encountered in practice. It tests for the kinds of knowledge, skills, and abilities required of an entry-level architect, with particular emphasis on those services that affect public health, safety, and welfare. In order to accomplish these objectives, the exam tests for

- knowledge in specific subject areas
- the ability to make decisions
- the ability to consolidate and use information to solve a problem
- the ability to coordinate the activities of others on the building team

The ARE also includes some professional practice and project management questions.

The ARE is based on particular editions of codes as specified in *ARE Guidelines*. These are not necessarily the most current editions. The material taken from the AISC 9th ed. *Manual of Steel Construction* may be out of date and has been replaced in more recent publications by AISC.

The ARE is developed jointly by the National Council of Architectural Registration Boards (NCARB) and the Committee of Canadian Architectural Councils (CCAC), with the assistance of the Chauncey Group International and Prometric. The Chauncey Group serves as NCARB's test development and operations consultant, and Prometric operates and maintains the test centers where the ARE is administered.

Although the responsibility of professional licensing rests with each individual state, every state's board requires successful completion of the ARE to achieve registration or licensure. One of the primary reasons for a uniform test is to facilitate reciprocity—that is, to enable an architect to more easily gain a license to practice in states other than the one in which he or she was originally licensed.

The ARE is administered and graded entirely by computer. All divisions of the exam are offered six days a week at a network of test centers across North America. The results are scored by computer, and the results are forwarded to individual state boards of architecture, which process them and send them to candidates. If you fail a division, you must wait six months before you can retake that division.

First Steps

As you begin to prepare for the exam, you should first obtain a current copy of *ARE Guidelines* from NCARB. This booklet will get you started with the exam process and will be a valuable reference throughout. It includes descriptions of the seven divisions, instructions on how to apply, pay for, and take the ARE, and other useful information. You can download a PDF version at www.ncarb.org, or you can request a printed copy through the contact information provided at that site.

The NCARB website also gives current information about the exam, education requirements, training, examination procedures, and NCARB reciprocity services. It includes sample scenarios of the computer-based examination process and examples of costs associated with taking the computer-based exam.

The PPI website is also a good source of exam info (at **www.ppi2pass.com/areinfo**) and answers to frequently asked questions (at **www.ppi2pass.com/arefaq**).

To register as an examinee, you should obtain the registration requirements from the board in the state, province, or territory where you want to be registered. The exact requirements vary from one jurisdiction to another, so contact your local board. Links to state boards can be found at **www.ppi2pass.com/areinfo**.

As soon as NCARB has verified your qualifications and you have received your "Authorization to Test" letter, you may begin scheduling examinations. The exams are offered on a first come, first served basis and must be scheduled at least 72 hours in advance. See *ARE Guidelines* for instructions on finding a current list of testing centers. You may take the exams at any location, even outside the state in which you intend to become registered.

You may schedule any division of the ARE at any time and may take the divisions in any order. Divisions can be taken one at a time, to spread out preparation time and exam costs, or can be taken together in any combination.

However, each candidate must pass all seven divisions of the ARE within a single five-year period. This period, or "rolling clock," begins on the date of the first division you passed. If you have not completed the ARE within five years, the divisions that you passed more than five years ago are no longer credited, and the content in them must be retaken. Your new five-year period begins on the date of the earliest division you passed within the last five years.

About the ARE 4.0

NCARB's introduction of ARE version 4.0 in July 2008 marked the change to an exam format with both multiple-choice and graphic subjects appearing within the same division. In the previous version, the ARE 3.1, each division contained either multiple-choice problems or graphic problems, never both.

The ARE 4.0 also has fewer divisions than the ARE 3.1, seven instead of nine. The organization of the ARE 4.0 exam means that candidates will make fewer trips to the test center, and can study for related portions of the exam all at once.

Examination Format

The ARE 4.0 is organized into seven divisions that test various areas of architectural knowledge and problem-solving ability.

Programming, Planning & Practice

> 85 multiple-choice questions
> 1 graphic vignette: Site Zoning

Site Planning & Design

> 65 multiple-choice questions
> 2 graphic vignettes: Site Design, Site Grading

Schematic Design

> 2 graphic vignettes: Building Layout, Interior Layout

Structural Systems

> 125 multiple-choice questions
> 1 graphic vignette: Structural Layout

Building Systems

95 multiple-choice questions
1 graphic vignette: Mechanical & Electrical Plan

Building Design & Construction Systems

85 multiple-choice questions
3 graphic vignettes: Accessibility/Ramp, Roof Plan, Stair Design

Construction Documents & Services

100 multiple-choice questions
1 graphic vignette: Building Section

Experienced test-takers will tell you that there is quite a bit of overlap among these divisions. Questions that seem better suited to the Construction Documents & Services division may show up on the Building Design & Construction Systems division, for example, and questions on architectural history and building regulations might show up anywhere. That's why it's important to have a comprehensive strategy for studying and taking the exams.

The ARE is given entirely by computer. There are two kinds of problems on the exam. Multiple-choice problems are short questions presented on the computer screen; you answer them by clicking on the right answer or answers, or by filling in a blank. Graphic vignettes are longer problems in design; you solve a vignette by planning and drawing your solution on the computer. Six of the seven divisions contain both multiple-choice sections and graphic vignettes; the Schematic Design division contains only vignettes. Both kinds of problems are described later in this Introduction.

STUDY GUIDELINES

After the five to seven years (or even more) of higher education you've received to this point, you probably have a good idea of the study strategy that works best for you. The trick is figuring out how to apply that to the ARE. Unlike many college courses, there isn't a textbook or set of class notes from which all the exam questions will be derived. The exams are very broad and draw questions from multiple areas of knowledge.

The first challenge, then, is figuring out what to study. The ARE is never quite the same exam twice. The field of knowledge tested is always the same, but the specific questions asked are drawn randomly from a large pool, and will differ from one candidate to the next. One division may contains many code-related questions for one candidate and only a few for the next. This makes the ARE a challenge to study for.

ARE Guidelines contains lists of resources recommended by NCARB. That list can seem overwhelming, though, and on top of that, many of the recommended books are expensive or no longer in print. To help address this problem, a number of publishers sell study guides for the ARE. These guides summarize the information found in primary sources such as the NCARB-recommended books. A list of helpful resources for preparing for the Structural Systems division can also be found in the Recommended Reading section of this book.

Your method of studying for the ARE should be based on both the content and form of the exam and on your school and work experience. Because the exam covers such a broad range of subject matter, it cannot possibly include every detail of practice. Rather, it tends to focus on what is considered entry-level knowledge and knowledge that is important for the protection of the public's health, safety, and welfare. Other types of questions are asked, too, but this knowledge should be the focus of your review schedule.

Your recent work experience should also help you determine what areas to study the most. A candidate who has been involved with construction documents for several years will probably need less review in that area than in others he or she has not had recent experience with.

The *ARE Review Manual* and its companion volumes are structured to help candidates focus on the topics that are more likely to be included in the exam in one form or another. Some subjects may seem familiar or may be easy to recall from memory, and others may seem completely foreign; the latter are the ones to give particular attention to. It may be wise to study additional sources on these subjects, take review seminars, or get special help from someone who is knowledgeable in the topic.

A typical candidate might spend about forty hours preparing for and taking each exam. Some will need to study more, some less. Forty hours is about one week of studying eight hours a day, or two weeks of four hours a day, or a month of two hours a day, along with reasonable breaks and time to attend to other responsibilities. As you probably work full time and have other family and personal obligations, it is important to develop a realistic schedule and do your best to stick to it. The ARE is not the kind of exam you can cram for the night before.

Also, since the fees are high and retaking a test is expensive, you want to do your best and pass in as few tries as possible. Allowing enough time to study and going into each exam well prepared will help you relax and concentrate on the questions.

The following steps may provide a useful structure for an exam study program.

Step 1: Start early. You can't review for a test like this by starting two weeks before the date. This is especially true if you are taking all portions of the exam for the first time.

Step 2: Go through the *ARE Review Manual* quickly to get a feeling for the scope of the subject matter and how the major topics are organized. Whatever division you're studying for, plan to review the chapters on building regulations as well. Review *ARE Guidelines*.

Step 3: Based on your review of the *ARE Review Manual* and *ARE Guidelines*, and on a realistic appraisal of your strong and weak areas, set priorities for study and determine which topics need more study time.

Step 4: Divide review subjects into manageable units and organize them into a sequence of study. It is generally best to start with the less familiar subjects. Based on the exam date and plans for beginning study, assign a time limit to each study unit. Again, your knowledge of a subject should determine the time devoted to it. You may want to devote an entire week to earthquake design if it is an unfamiliar subject, and only one day to timber design if it is a familiar one. In setting up a schedule, be realistic about other life commitments as well as your personal ability to concentrate on studying over a length of time.

Step 5: Begin studying, and stick with the schedule. Of course, this is the most difficult part of the process and the one that requires the most self-discipline. The job should be easier if you have started early and if you are following a realistic schedule that allows time for recreation and personal commitments.

Step 6: Stop studying a day or two before the exam. Relax. By this time, no amount of additional cramming will help.

At some point in your studying, you will want to spend some time becoming familiar with the program you will be using to solve the graphic vignettes, which does not resemble commercial CAD software. The software and sample vignettes can be downloaded from the NCARB website at www.ncarb.org.

There are many schools of thought on the best order for taking the divisions. One factor to consider is the six-month waiting period before you can retake a particular division. It's never fun to predict what you might fail, but if you know that a specific area might give you trouble, consider taking that exam near the beginning. You might be pleasantly surprised when you check the mailbox, but if not, as you work through the rest of the exams, the clock will be ticking and you can schedule the retest six months later.

Here are some additional tips.

- Learn concepts first, and then details later. For example, it is much better to understand the basic ideas and theories of waterproofing than it is to attempt to memorize dozens of waterproofing products and details. Once the concept is clear, the details are much easier to learn and to apply during the exam.

- Use the index to the *ARE Review Manual* to focus on particular subjects in which you feel weak, especially subjects that can apply to more than one division.

- Don't tackle all your hardest subjects first. Make one of your early exams one that you feel fairly confident about. It's nice to get off on the right foot with a PASS.

- Programming, Planning & Practice and Building Design & Construction Systems both tend to be "catch-all" divisions that cover a lot of material from the Construction Documents & Services division as well as others. Consider taking Construction Documents & Services first among those three, and then the other two soon after.

- Many past candidates recommend taking the Programming, Planning & Practice division last or nearly last, so that you will be familiar with the body of knowledge for all the other divisions as well.

- Brush up on architectural history before taking any of the divisions with multiple-choice sections. Know major buildings and their architects, particularly structures that are representative of an architect's philosophy (for example, Le Corbusier and the Villa Savoye) or that represent "firsts" or "turning points."

- Try to schedule your exams so that you'll have enough time to get yourself ready, eat, and review a little. If you'll have a long drive to the testing center, try to avoid having to make it during rush hour.

- If you are planning to take more than one division at a time, do not overstudy any one portion of the exam. It is generally better to review the concepts than to try to become an overnight expert in one area. For example, the exam may ask general questions about plate girders, but it will not ask for a complete, detailed design of a plate girder.

- Solve as many sample problems as possible, including those provided with NCARB's practice program, the books of sample problems and practice exams published by PPI, and any others that are available.

- Take advantage of the community of intern architects going through this experience with you. Some local AIA chapters offer ARE preparation courses or may be able to help you organize a study group with other interns in your area. Visit website forums to discuss the exam with others who have taken it or are preparing to take it. The Architecture Exam Forum at **www.ppi2pass.com/areforum** is a great online resource for questions, study advice, and encouragement. Even though the ARE questions change daily, it is a good idea to get a feeling for the types of questions that are being asked, the general emphasis, and the subject areas that previous candidates have found particularly troublesome.

- A day or two before the first test session, stop studying in order to relax as much as possible. Get plenty of sleep the night before the test.

- Try to relax as much as possible during study periods and during the exam itself. Worrying is counterproductive. Candidates who have worked diligently in school, have obtained a wide range of experience during internship, and have started exam review early will be in the best possible position to pass the ARE.

TAKING THE EXAM

What to Bring

Bring multiple forms of photo ID and your Authorization to Test letter to the test site.

It is neither necessary nor permitted to bring any reference materials or scratch paper into the test site. Pencils and scratch paper are provided by the proctor and must be returned when leaving the exam room. Earplugs will also be provided. Leave all your books and notes in the car. Most testing centers have lockers for your keys, small personal belongings, and cell phone.

Do not bring a calculator into the test site. A calculator built into the testing software will be available in all divisions.

Arriving at the Testing Center

Allow plenty of time to get to the exam site, to avoid transportation problems such as getting lost or stuck in traffic jams. If you can, arrive a little early, and take a little time in the parking lot to review one last time the formulas and other things you need to memorize. Then relax, take a few deep breaths, and go take the exam.

Once at the testing center, you will check in with the attendant, who will verify your identification and your Authorization to Test. (Don't forget to take this home with you after each exam; you'll need it for the next one.) After you check in, you'll be shown to your testing station.

When the exam begins, you will have the opportunity to click through a tutorial that explains how the computer program works. You'll probably want to read through it the first time, but after that initial exam, you will know how the software works and you won't need the tutorial. Take a deep breath, organize your paper and pencils, and take advantage of the opportunity to dump all the facts floating around in your brain onto your scratch paper—write down as much as you can. This includes formulas, ratios ("if x increases, y decreases"), and so on—anything that you are trying desperately not to forget. If you can get all the things you've crammed at the last minute onto that paper, you'll be able to think a little more clearly about the questions posed on the screen.

Taking the Multiple-Choice Sections

The ARE multiple-choice sections include several types of questions.

One type of multiple-choice question is based on written, graphic, or photographic information. The candidate examines the information and selects the correct answer from four given answer choices. Some problems may require calculations.

A second type of multiple-choice question lists four or five items or statements, which are given Roman numerals from I to IV or I to V. For example, the question may give five statements about a subject, and the candidate must choose the statements that are true. The four answer choices are combinations of these numerals, such as "I and III" or "II, IV, and V".

A third type of multiple-choice question describes a situation that could be encountered in actual practice. Drawings, diagrams, photographs, forms, tables, or other data may also be given. The question asks the examinee to select the best answer from four options.

Two kinds of questions that NCARB calls "alternate item types" also show up in the multiple-choice sections. In a "fill in the blank" question, the examinee must fill a blank with a number derived from a table or calculation. In a "check all that apply" question, six answer choices are given, and the candidate must choose all the correct answers. The question tells how many of the choices are correct, from two to four. The examinee must choose all the correct answers to receive credit; partial credit is not given.

Between 10% and 15% of the questions in a multiple-choice section will be these "alternate item type" questions. Every question on the ARE, however, counts the same toward your total score.

Keep in mind that multiple-choice questions often require the examinee to do more than just select an answer based on memory. At times it will be necessary to combine several facts, analyze data, perform a calculation, or review a drawing. Remember, too, that most candidates do not need the entire time allotted for the multiple-choice sections. If you have time for more than one pass through the questions, you can make good use of it.

Here are some tips for the multiple-choice problems.

- Go through the entire section in one somewhat swift pass, answering the questions that you're sure about and marking the others so you can return to them later. If a question requires calculations, skip it for now unless it's very simple. Then go back to the beginning and work your way through the exam again, taking a little more time to read each question and think through the answer.

- Another benefit of going through the entire section at the beginning is that occasionally there is information in one question that may help you answer another question somewhere else.

- If you are very unsure of a question, pick your best answer choice, mark it, and move on. You will probably have time at the end of the test to go back and recheck these answers. But remember, your first response is usually the best.

- Always answer all the questions. Unanswered questions are counted wrong, so even if you are just guessing, it's better to choose an answer and have a chance of it being correct than to skip it and be certain of getting it wrong. When faced with four answer choices, the old SAT strategy of eliminating the two answers that are definitely wrong and making your best guess between the two that remain is helpful on the ARE, too.

- Some questions may seem too simple. Although a few very easy and obvious questions are included on the ARE, more often the simplicity should serve as a red flag to warn you to reevaluate the question for exceptions to a rule or special circumstances that make the obvious, easy response incorrect.

- Watch out for absolute words in a question, such as "always," "never," and "completely." These are often a clue that some little exception exists, turning what reads like a true statement into a false one or vice versa.

- Be alert for words like "seldom," "usually," "best," and "most reasonable." These indicate that some judgment will be involved in answering the question. Look for two or more options that appear to be very similar.

- Some divisions will provide an on-screen reference sheet with useful formulas and other information that will help you solve some problems. Skim through the reference sheet so you know what information is there, and then use it as a resource.

- Occasionally there may be a defective question. This does not happen very often, but if it does, make the best choice possible under the circumstances. Flawed questions are usually discovered, and either they are not counted on the test or any one of the correct answers is credited.

Solving the Vignettes

Each of the eleven graphic vignettes on the ARE is designed to test a particular area of knowledge and skill. Each one presents a base plan of some kind and gives programmatic and other requirements. The candidate must create a plan that satisfies the requirements.

In the Structural Layout vignette, the candidate is given the floor plan of a small building and must sketch a structural system that meets certain requirements. The structural system includes columns, bearing walls, and the roof structure. The spacing of beams and joists must be reasonable for the spans and layout of the building. All elements of structural continuity must be shown so that loads are carried from the roof to the foundation.

The computer scores the vignettes by a complex grading method. Design criteria are given various point values, and responses are categorized as Acceptable, Unacceptable, or Indeterminate.

General Tips for the Vignettes

Here are some general tips for approaching the vignettes. More detailed solving tips can be found in the vignette solutions in this book.

- Remember that with the current format and computer grading, each vignette covers only a very specific area of knowledge and offers a limited number of possible solutions. In a few cases only one solution is really possible. Use this as an advantage.

- Read the problem thoroughly, twice. Follow the requirements exactly, letting each problem solve itself as much as possible. Be careful not to read more into the problem than is there. The test writers are very specific about what they want; there is no need to add to the problem requirements. If a particular type of solution is strongly suggested, follow that lead.

- Consider only those code requirements given in the vignette, even if they deviate from familiar codes. Do not read anything more into the problem. The code requirements may be slightly different from what candidates use in practice.

- Use the scratch paper provided to sketch possible solutions before starting the final solution.

- Make sure all programmed elements are included in the final design.

- When the functional requirements of the problem have been solved, use the problem statement as a checklist to make sure all criteria have been satisfied.

General Tips for Using the Vignette Software

It is important to practice with the vignette software that will be used in the exam. The program is unique to the ARE and unlike standard CAD software. If you are unfamiliar with the software interface you will waste valuable time learning to use it, and are likely to run out of time before completing the vignettes. Practice software can be downloaded at no charge from NCARB's website at www.ncarb.org. Usage time for the practice program can also be purchased at Prometric test centers. The practice software includes tutorials, directions, and one practice vignette for each of the eleven vignettes.

Here are some general tips for using the vignette software.

- When elements overlap on the screen, it may be difficult to select a particular element. If this happens, repeatedly click on the element without moving the mouse until the desire element is highlighted.

- Try to stay in "ortho" mode. This mode can be used to solve most problems, and it makes the solution process much easier and quicker. Unless obviously required by the vignette, creating additional angles complicates any problem with the time restrictions given.

- If the vignette relates to contour modifications, it may help to draw schematic sections through the significant existing slopes. This provides a three-dimensional image of the problem.

- When drawing, if the program states that elements should connect, make sure they touch at their boundaries only and do not overlap. Use the *check* tool to determine if there are any overlaps. Walls that do not align correctly can cause a solution to be downgraded or even rejected. Remember, walls between spaces change color temporarily when properly aligned.

- Make liberal use of the *zoom* tool for sizing and aligning components accurately. Zoom in as closely as possible on the area being worked. When aligning objects, it is also helpful to use the full-screen cursor.

- Turn on the grid and verify spacing. This makes it easier to align objects and get a sense of the sizes of objects and the distances between them. Use the *measure* tool to check exact measurements if needed.

- Make liberal use of the sketch tools. These can be turned on and off and do not count during the grading, but they can be used to show relationships and for temporary guidelines and other notations.

- Use sketch circles to show required distances, setbacks, clearances, and similar measures.

AFTER THE EXAM

When you've clicked the button to end the test, the computer may prompt you to provide some demographic information about yourself and your education and experience. Then gather your belongings, turn in your scratch paper and materials—you must leave them with the proctor—and leave the testing center. (For security reasons, you can't remove anything from the test center.) If the staff has retained your Authorization to Test and your identification, don't forget to retrieve both.

If you should encounter any problems during the exams or have any concerns, be sure to report them to the test center administrator and to NCARB as soon as possible. If you wait longer than ten days after you test, NCARB will not respond to your complaint. You must report your complaint immediately and directly to NCARB and copy your state registration board for any hope of assistance.

Then it's all over but the wait for the mail. How long it takes to get your scores will vary with the efficiency of your state registration board, which reviews the scores from NCARB before passing along the results. But four to six weeks is typical.

As you may have heard from classmates and colleagues, the ARE is a difficult exam—but it is certainly not impossible to pass. A solid architectural education and a well-rounded internship are the best preparation you can have. Watch carefully and listen to the vocabulary used by architects with more experience. Look for opportunities to participate in all phases of project delivery so that you have some "real world" experience to apply to the scenarios you will inevitably find in exam questions.

One last piece of advice is not to put off taking the exams. Take them as soon as you become eligible. You will probably still remember a little bit from your college courses and

you may even have your old textbooks and notes handy. As
life gets more complicated—with spouses and children and
work obligations—it is easy to make excuses and never find
time to get around to it. Make the commitment, and do it
now. After all, this is the last step to reaching your goal of
calling yourself an architect.

PROFESSIONAL PUBLICATIONS, INC.

HOW TO USE THIS BOOK

This book contains 125 sample multiple-choice problems and one sample vignette, as well as one complete practice exam consisting of 125 multiple-choice problems and one vignette. These have been written to help you prepare for the Structural Systems division of the Architect Registration Examination, version 4.0.

One of the best ways to prepare for the ARE is by solving sample problems. While you are studying for this division, use the sample problems in this book to make yourself familiar with the different types of questions and the breadth of topics you are likely to encounter on the actual exam. Then when it's time to take the ARE, you will already be comfortable with the format of the exam questions. Also, seeing which sample problems you can and cannot answer correctly will help you gauge your understanding of the topics covered in the Structural Systems division.

The sample multiple-choice problems in this book are organized by subject area, so that you can concentrate on one subject at a time if you like. Each problem is immediately followed by its answer and an explanation.

Several of the problems will require you to refer to the figures and tables in the Appendix of this book, which begins on page 101.

The sample vignette in this book can be solved directly on the base plan provided or on a sheet of tracing paper. Alternatively, you can download an electronic file of the base plan in PDF format from **www.ppi2pass.com/vignettes** for use in your own CAD program. (On the actual exam, vignettes are solved on the computer using NCARB's own software; see the Introduction for more information about this.) When you are finished with your solution to the vignette, compare it against the sample passing and failing solutions that follow.

While the sample problems in this book are intended for you to use as you study for the exam, the practice exam is best used only when you have almost finished your study of the Structural Systems topics. A week or two before you are scheduled to take the division, when you feel you are nearly ready for the exam, do a "dry run" by taking the practice exam in this book. This will hone your test-taking skills and give you a reality check about how prepared you really are.

The experience will be most valuable to you if you treat the practice exam as though it were an actual exam. Do not read the questions ahead of time and do not look at the solutions until after you've finished. Try to simulate the exam experience as closely as possible. This means locking yourself away in a quiet space, setting an alarm for the exam's testing time, and working through the entire examination with no coffee, television, or telephone—only your calculator, a pencil, your drafting tools or CAD program for the vignette, and a few sheets of scratch paper. (On the actual exam, these are provided.) This will help you prepare to budget your time, give you an idea of what the actual exam experience will be like, and help you develop a test-taking strategy that works for you.

The target times for the sections of the practice exam are

Multiple choice: 3.5 hours

Structural Layout vignette: 1 hour

Record your answers for the multiple-choice section of the practice exam using the "bubble" answer form at the front of the exam. When you are finished, you can check your answers quickly against the filled-in answer key at the front of the Solutions section. Then turn to the solutions and read the explanations of the answers, especially those you answered incorrectly. The explanation will give you a better understanding of the intent of the question and why individual choices are right or wrong.

The Solutions section may also be used as a guide for the final phase of your studies. As opposed to a traditional study guide that is organized into chapters and paragraphs of facts, this question-and-answer format can help you see how the exam might address a topic, and what types of questions you are likely to encounter. If you still are not clear about a particular subject after reading a solution's explanation, review the subject in one of your study resources. Give yourself time for further study, and then take the multiple-choice section again.

The vignette portion of the practice exam can be solved the same way as the sample vignette, either directly on the base plans, on tracing paper, or with a CAD program using the electronic file downloaded from **www.ppi2pass.com/vignettes**. Try to solve the vignette within the target time given. When you are finished, compare your drawing against the passing and failing solutions given in the Solutions section.

This book is best used in conjunction with your primary study source or study guide, such as PPI's *ARE Review Manual*. *Structural Systems: ARE Sample Problems and Practice Exam* is not intended to give you all the information you will need to pass this division of the ARE. Rather, it is designed to expose you to a variety of problem types and to help you sharpen your problem-solving and test-taking skills. With a sound review and the practice you'll get from this book, you'll be well on your way to successfully passing the Structural Systems division of the Architect Registration Examination.

HOW SI UNITS ARE USED IN THIS BOOK

This book includes equivalent measurements in the text and illustrations using the Système International (SI), or the metric system as it is commonly called. However, the use of SI units for construction and book publishing in the United States is problematic. This is because the building construction industry in the United States (with the exception of federal construction) has generally not adopted the metric system. As a result, equivalent measurements of customary U.S. units (also called English or inch-pound units) are usually given as a *soft* conversion, in which customary U.S. measurements are simply converted into SI units using standard conversion factors. This always results in a number with excessive significant digits. When construction is done using SI units, the building is designed and drawn according to *hard* conversions, where planning dimensions and building products are based on a metric module from the beginning. For example, studs are spaced 400 mm on center to accommodate panel products that are manufactured in standard 1200 mm widths.

During the present time of transition to the Système International in the United States, code-writing bodies, federal laws such as the ADA, product manufacturers, trade associations, and other construction-related industries typically still use the customary U.S. system and make soft conversions to develop SI equivalents. In the case of some product manufacturers, they produce the same product using both measuring systems. Although there are industry standards for developing SI equivalents, there is no perfect consistency for rounding off when conversions are made. For example, the International Building Code shows a 152 mm equivalent when a 6 in dimension is required, while the Americans with Disabilities Act Accessibility Guidelines (ADAAG) give a 150 mm equivalent for the same customary U.S. dimension.

To further complicate matters, each book publisher may employ a slightly different house style in handling SI equivalents when customary U.S. units are used as the primary measuring system. The confusion is likely to continue until the United States construction industry adopts the SI system completely, eliminating the need for dual dimensioning in publishing.

For the purposes of this book, the following conventions have been adopted.

Throughout the book, the customary U.S. measurements are given first with the SI equivalent shown in parentheses. When the measurement is millimeters, units are not shown. For example, a dimension may be indicated as 4 ft 8 in (1422). When the SI equivalent is some other unit, such as for volume or area, the units are indicated. For example, 250 ft² (23 m²).

Following standard conventions, all SI distance measurements in illustrations are in millimeters unless specifically indicated as meters.

When a measurement is given as part of a problem scenario, the SI measurement is not necessarily meant to be roughly equal to the U.S. measurement. For example, a hypothetical force on a beam might be given as 12 kips (12 kN). 12 kips is actually equal to about 53.38 kN, but the intention in such cases is only to provide two problems, one in U.S. units and one in SI units, of about the same difficulty. Solve the entire problem in either U.S. or SI units; don't try to convert from one to the other in the middle of solving a problem.

When dimensions are for informational use, the SI equivalent rounded to the nearest millimeter is used.

When dimensions are given and they relate to planning or design guidelines, the SI equivalent is rounded to the nearest 5 mm for numbers over a few inches and to the nearest 10 mm for numbers over a few feet. When the dimension exceeds several feet, the number is rounded to the nearest 100 mm. For example, if you need a space about 10 ft wide for a given activity, the modular, rounded SI equivalent will be given as 3000 mm. More exact conversions are not required.

When an item is only manufactured to a customary U.S. measurement, the nearest SI equivalent rounded to the nearest millimeter is given, unless the dimension is very small (as for metal gages), in which case a more precise decimal equivalent will be given. Some materials, such as glass, are often manufactured to SI sizes. So, for example, a nominal $^1\!/_2$ in thick piece of glass will have an SI equivalent of 13 mm but can be ordered as 12 mm.

When there is a hard conversion in the industry and an SI equivalent item is manufactured, the hard conversion is given. For example, a 24 × 24 ceiling tile would have the hard conversion of 600 × 600 (instead of 610) because these are manufactured and available in the United States.

When an SI conversion is used by a code agency, such as the International Building Code (IBC), or published in another regulation, such as the ADA Accessibility Guidelines, the SI equivalents used by the issuing agency are printed in this book. For example, the same 10 ft dimension given previously as 3000 mm for a planning guideline would have an SI equivalent of 3048 mm in the context of the IBC because this is what that code requires. The ADA Accessibility Guidelines generally follow the rounding rule, to take SI dimensions to the nearest 10 mm. For example, a 10 ft requirement for accessibility will be shown as 3050 mm. The code requirements for readers outside the United States may be slightly different.

This book uses different abbreviations for pounds of force and pounds of mass in customary U.S. units. The abbreviation used for pounds of force (pounds-force) is lbf, and the abbreviation used for pounds of mass (pounds-mass) is lbm.

CODES AND STANDARDS USED IN THIS BOOK

American Concrete Institute. *Building Code Requirements for Reinforced Concrete (ACI 318) and Commentary*, 2005 ed. Detroit, MI.

American Forest & Paper Association. *National Design Specification® for Wood Construction, ASD/LRFD*, 2005 ed. Washington, DC.

American Institute of Steel Construction. *Manual of Steel Construction, Allowable Stress Design*, 9th ed. Chicago, IL.

American Society of Civil Engineers. *Minimum Design Loads for Buildings and Other Structures, ASCE Standard (ASCE/SEI 7)*, 2005 ed. Reston, VA.

International Code Council. *International Building Code*, 2006 ed. Washington, DC.

RECOMMENDED READING

General Reference

Access Board. *ADAAG Manual: A Guide to the Americans with Disabilities Accessibility Guidelines*. East Providence, RI: BNI Building News.

_____. *ADAAG Manual: Americans with Disabilities Act Accessibility Guidelines for Buildings and Facilities*. Washington, DC: U.S. Architectural and Transportation Barriers Compliance Board. www.access-board.gov/adaag/html/adaag.htm.

ARCOM. *MASTERSPEC*. Salt Lake City: ARCOM. (Familiarity with the format and language of specifications is very helpful.)

ARCOM and American Institute of Architects. *The Graphic Standards Guide to Architectural Finishes: Using Masterspec® to Evaluate, Select, and Specify Materials*. New York: John Wiley & Sons.

Ballast, David Kent, and Steven O'Hara. *ARE Review Manual*. Belmont, CA: PPI.

Canadian Commission on Building and Fire Codes. *National Building Code of Canada*. Ottawa: National Research Council of Canada.

Fitch, James Marston. *Historic Preservation: Curatorial Management of the Built World*. Charlottesville: University Press of Virginia.

Guthrie, Pat. *Architect's Portable Handbook*. New York: McGraw-Hill.

Harris, Cyril M., ed. *Dictionary of Architecture and Construction*. New York: McGraw-Hill.

International Code Council. *International Building Code*. Washington, DC: International Code Council.

_____. *Standard on Accessible and Usable Buildings and Facilities* (ICC/ANSI A117.1). Washington, DC: American National Standards Institute, International Code Council.

Patterson, Terry L. *Illustrated 2000 Building Code Handbook*. New York: McGraw-Hill.

Ramsey, Charles G., and Harold R. Sleeper. *Architectural Graphic Standards*. New York: John Wiley & Sons. (The student edition is an acceptable substitute for the professional version.)

U.S. Green Building Council. *LEED Reference Package for New Construction and Major Renovations*. Washington, DC: U.S. Green Building Council.

Structural Systems: General Structures

Al-Manaseer, Akthem, and Nadim M. Hassoun. *Structural Concrete: Theory and Design*. New York, NY: John Wiley & Sons.

Ambrose, James. *Simplified Design of Steel Structures*. New York, NY: John Wiley & Sons.

_____. *Simplified Design of Wood Structures*. New York, NY: John Wiley & Sons.

_____. *Simplified Engineering for Architects and Builders*. New York, NY: John Wiley & Sons.

_____. *Simplified Mechanics and Strength of Materials*. New York, NY: John Wiley & Sons.

Bassin, Milton, Stanley Brodsky, and Harold Wolkoff. *Statics and Strength of Materials*. New York, NY: McGraw-Hill.

Breyer, Donald. *Design of Wood Structures*, New York, NY: McGraw-Hill Professional.

Chiuini, Michele, and Rod Underwood. *Structural Design: A Practical Guide for Architects*. New York, NY: John Wiley & Sons.

Cooper, Sol E., and Andrew C. Chen. *Designing Steel Structures: Methods and Cases*. Englewood Cliffs, NJ: Prentice Hall.

Crawley, Stanley W., and Robert M. Dillon. *Steel Buildings: Analysis and Design*. New York, NY: John Wiley & Sons.

Galambos, Theodore V., and Bruce G. Johnston. *Basic Steel Design with LRFD*. Upper Saddle River, NJ: Prentice Hall.

Hibbeler, R.C. *Structural Analysis*. Upper Saddle River, NJ: Prentice Hall.

McCormac, Jack C., and James K. Nelson. *Design of Reinforced Concrete, ACI 318-05 Code Edition*. New York, NY: John Wiley & Sons.

Salmon, Charles G., and Chu-Kia Wang. *Reinforced Concrete Design*. New York, NY: John Wiley & Sons.

Shaeffer, R.E. *Reinforced Concrete: Preliminary Design for Architects and Builders*. Tallahassee, FL: Textbooks, Ltd.

Somayaji, Shan. *Structural Wood Design*. St. Paul, MN: West Publishing Company.

Vinnakota, Sriramulu. *Steel Structures: Behavior and LRFD*. New York, NY: McGraw-Hill.

Structural Systems: Lateral Forces

Ambrose, James. *Simplified Design of Steel Structures*. New York, NY: John Wiley & Sons.

———. *Simplified Design of Wood Structures*. New York, NY: John Wiley & Sons.

Breyer, Donald. *Design of Wood Structures*. New York, NY: McGraw-Hill Professional.

Chiuini, Michele, and Rod Underwood. *Structural Design: A Practical Guide for Architects*. New York, NY: John Wiley & Sons.

Cooper, Sol E., and Andrew C. Chen. *Designing Steel Structures: Methods and Cases*. Englewood Cliffs, NJ: Prentice Hall.

Crawley, Stanley W,. and Robert M. Dillon. *Steel Buildings: Analysis and Design*. New York, NY: John Wiley & Sons.

Somayaji, Shan. *Structural Wood Design*. St. Paul, MN: West Publishing Company.

Graphic Vignettes

Allen, Edward, and Joseph Iano. *The Architect's Studio Companion: Rules of Thumb for Preliminary Design*. New York: John Wiley & Sons.

Ambrose, James, and Peter Brandow. *Simplified Site Design*. New York: John Wiley & Sons.

Ching, Francis D. K., and Steven R. Winkel. *Building Codes Illustrated: A Guide to Understanding the International Building Code*. New York: John Wiley & Sons.

Hoke, John Ray, ed. *Architectural Graphic Standards*. New York: John Wiley & Sons.

Karlen, Mark. *Space Planning Basics*. New York: John Wiley & Sons.

Parker, Harry, John W. MacGuire, and James Ambrose. *Simplified Site Engineering*. New York: John Wiley & Sons.

Architectural History

(Brush up on this before taking any of the multiple-choice exams, as architectural history questions are scattered throughout the sections.)

Curtis, William J.R. *Modern Architecture Since 1900*. London: Phaedon Press, Ltd.

Frampton, Kenneth. *Modern Architecture: A Critical History*. London: Thames and Hudson.

Trachtenberg, Marvin, and Isabelle Hyman. *Architecture: From Pre-History to Post-Modernism*. Englewood Cliffs, NJ: Prentice-Hall.

SAMPLE PROBLEMS

STATICS AND STRENGTH OF MATERIALS

1. Find the direction and magnitude of the resultant (R) of the three concurrent forces shown. θ is the angle of the resultant measured counterclockwise from horizontal x-axis.

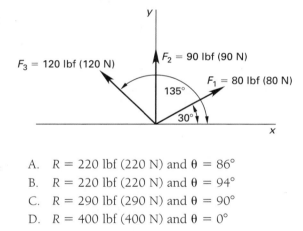

A. $R = 220$ lbf (220 N) and $\theta = 86°$
B. $R = 220$ lbf (220 N) and $\theta = 94°$
C. $R = 290$ lbf (290 N) and $\theta = 90°$
D. $R = 400$ lbf (400 N) and $\theta = 0°$

Solution

Use the component summation method to find the resultant (R) of the three concurrent forces. Resolve each force (F) into two rectangular components in the rectangular coordinate system.

$$F_x = F \cos \theta$$

$$F_y = F \sin \theta$$

θ is the angle that each force makes with the horizontal x-axis.

force, F (lbf or N)	angle, θ (°)	$F_x = F \cos \theta$ (lbf or N)	$F_y = F \sin \theta$ (lbf or N)
80	30	$(80)(0.866) = 69.3$	$(80)(0.5) = 40$
90	90	$(90)(0) = 0$	$(90)(1) = 90$
120	135	$(120)(-0.707) = -84.9$	$(120)(0.707) = 84.9$

The rectangular components of the resultant are

$$R_x = \Sigma F_x$$
$$= 69.3 + 0 - 84.9$$
$$= -15.6$$
$$R_y = \Sigma F_y$$
$$= 40 + 90 + 84.9$$
$$= 214.9$$

The magnitude of the resultant is

$$R = \sqrt{R_x^2 + R_y^2}$$

$$= \sqrt{(-15.6)^2 + (214.9)^2}$$

$$= 215.47 \quad (220)$$

The angle of the resultant is found from the equation

$$\tan \theta = \frac{R_y}{R_x}$$

$$\theta = \tan^{-1} \frac{R_y}{R_x} = \tan^{-1} \frac{214.9}{-15.6}$$

$$\theta = -85.85° \quad (-86°)$$

The angle of –86° puts the resultant in the second quadrant, and is equivalent to an angle of 94° measured counterclockwise from the x-axis.

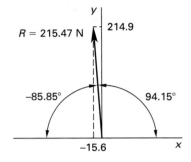

The answer is B.

2.   The moment of inertia for the cross section of a member is related to the

I.   shape of the cross section
II.   modulus of elasticity of the material
III. dimensions of the cross section
IV.   load applied on the member

    A.   I and II only
    B.   I and III only
    C.   I, II, and III only
    D.   II, III, and IV only

Solution

The moment of inertia of a cross section is a property of the section and not of the material the member is made of. Therefore, the moment of inertia is not related to the modulus of elasticity (II). The moment of inertia is also unrelated to the load applied on the member (IV). It depends only on the shape and dimensions (I and III).

The answer is B.

3.   The section modulus for the cross section of a member is related to the

I.   moment of inertia of the cross section
II.   depth of the cross section
III. bending stress in the member
IV.   modulus of elasticity of the member

    A.   I and II only
    B.   II and III only
    C.   I, II, and III only
    D.   II, III, and IV only

Solution

The section modulus (S) for the cross section of a member is the cross section's moment of inertia (I) divided by the distance from the cross section's neutral axis to its extreme fibers (c).

$$S = \frac{I}{c}$$

The section modulus is, therefore, related to the moment of inertia and the depth of the cross section (I and II). It is not related to the bending stress in the member (III), nor to the mechanical properties of the material such as the modulus of elasticity (IV).

The answer is A.

4.   Strain in a member is

    A.   the modulus of elasticity multiplied by the stress
    B.   the deflection of a beam due to loads
    C.   the applied load divided by the area
    D.   the deformation or change in size caused by external forces

Solution

Strain is the deformation or change in size caused by external forces applied on a member. It is an elongation under tensile forces and a shortening under compressive forces.

The modulus of elasticity is calculated by dividing stress by strain, so strain is equal to stress divided by the modulus of elasticity (rather than stress multiplied by the modulus of elasticity, as stated in choice A). The deflection of a beam (choice B) is how far the beam bends under a load. Stress, not strain, is calculated by dividing the load by the area (choice C).

The answer is D.

5.   A rod of AISI 1020 structural steel has a diameter of 3 in (80) and is subjected to a tension force of 75,000 lbf (150 000 N). The modulus of elasticity for AISI 1020 steel is 30×10^6 psi (200×10^3 MPa). What is the strain?

    A.   0.00035 in/in (0.000 15 mm/mm)

    B.   0.0035 in/in (0.0015 mm/mm)

    C.   3.5 in/in (0.015 mm/mm)

    D.   11 in/in (0.045 mm/mm)

Solution

Strain is equal to stress divided by the modulus of elasticity.

$$\epsilon = \frac{f}{E}$$

Stress is equal to force divided by the cross-sectional area.

$$f = \frac{F}{A}$$

In U.S. units:

The area is

$$A = \pi r^2 = \pi(1.5 \text{ in})^2 = 7.07 \text{ in}^2$$

Stress is

$$f = \frac{F}{A} = \frac{75,000 \text{ lbf}}{7.07 \text{ in}^2} = 10,600 \text{ lbf/in}^2$$

Strain is

$$\epsilon = \frac{f}{E} = \frac{10,600 \ \dfrac{\text{lbf}}{\text{in}^2}}{30 \times 10^6 \ \dfrac{\text{lbf}}{\text{in}^2}} = 0.00035 \text{ in/in}$$

In SI units:

The area is

$$A = \pi r^2 = \pi(40 \text{ mm})^2 = 5030 \text{ mm}^2$$

Stress is

$$f = \frac{F}{A} = \frac{150\,000 \text{ N}}{5030 \text{ mm}^2} = 29.8 \text{ MPa}$$

Strain is

$$\epsilon = \frac{f}{E} = \frac{29.8 \text{ MPa}}{200 \times 10^3 \text{ MPa}} = 0.000 \ 15 \text{ mm/mm}$$

The answer is A.

6.   For the T-section shown, what is the moment of inertia about the vertical centroidal axis?

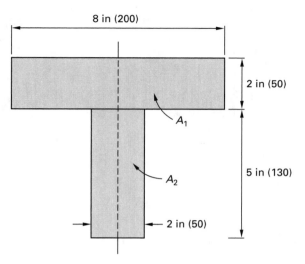

    A.   26 in^4 (1.1×10^7 mm^4)

    B.   89 in^4 (3.5×10^7 mm^4)

    C.   260 in^4 (1.1×10^8 mm^4)

    D.   2600 in^4 (1.1×10^9 mm^4)

Solution

The moment of inertia (I_y) for a rectangular area about its vertical centroidal axis is calculated by

$$I_y = \frac{bh^3}{12}$$

b is the dimension of the rectangle parallel to the axis, and h is the dimension perpendicular to the axis.

To calculate the total moment of inertia for the T-section about the vertical centroidal axis, separate the shape into two rectangular areas. Then, add together the individual moments of inertia.

In U.S. units:

$$I_{y, \text{ total}} = I_{y,A_1} + I_{y,A_2} = \frac{(2 \text{ in})(8 \text{ in})^3}{12} + \frac{(5 \text{ in})(2 \text{ in})^3}{12}$$

$$= 88.66 \text{ in}^4 \quad (89 \text{ in}^4)$$

In SI units:

$$I_{y, \text{ total}} = I_{y,A_1} + I_{y,A_2}$$

$$= \frac{(50 \text{ mm})(200 \text{ mm})^3}{12} + \frac{(130 \text{ mm})(50 \text{ mm})^3}{12}$$

$$= 3.49 \times 10^7 \text{ mm}^4 \quad (3.5 \times 10^7 \text{ mm}^4)$$

The answer is B.

7. A 10 ft (3 m) long cast-iron pipe is fastened between two walls. The coefficient of thermal linear expansion is 6.3×10^{-6} in/in-°F (11.3×10^{-6} mm/mm·°C), and the modulus of elasticity is 11×10^6 psi (75×10^3 MPa). What is the compressive stress in the pipe due to a temperature rise of 30°F (15°C)?

A. 2.1 psi (0.013 MPa)
B. 21 psi (0.13 MPa)
C. 2100 psi (13 MPa)
D. 21,000 psi (130 MPa)

Solution

The thermal stress is

$$s = E\alpha\Delta T$$

E is the modulus of elasticity, α is the coefficient of thermal linear expansion, and ΔT is the change in temperature.

In U.S. units:

$$s = \left(11 \times 10^6 \frac{\text{lbf}}{\text{in}^2}\right)\left(6.3 \times 10^{-6} \frac{\text{in}}{\text{in-°F}}\right)(30°F)$$

$$= 2079 \text{ lbf/in}^2 \quad (2080 \text{ psi})$$

In SI units:

$$s = (75 \times 10^3 \text{ MPa})\left(11.3 \times 10^{-6} \frac{\text{mm}}{\text{mm·°C}}\right)(15°C)$$

$$= 12.713 \text{ MPa} \quad (12.7 \text{ MPa})$$

The answer is C.

STRUCTURAL ANALYSIS

8. Which statement about beams and shear stress is true?

A. Beams often fail due to shear stress.
B. Shear stress in beams is seldom a problem, but it can be critical in short, heavily loaded spans.
C. Shear stress in beams is seldom a problem, but it can be critical in long spans carrying light loads.
D. In steel beams, the AISC limits shear stress to 60% of the yield stress.

Solution

Shear stress in beams is seldom a problem, and beams rarely fail due to shear. However, shear can become critical in beams with short, heavily loaded spans. The shear stress in steel beams is actually limited to 40% of the yield stress, according to the AISC Specification.

The answer is B.

9. By normal convention, when the top fibers of a rectangular beam are in tension and bottom fibers are in compression with the same magnitude as the tension, the bending moment is

A. positive
B. zero
C. negative
D. indeterminate

Solution

The bending moment in a beam is considered negative when the beam's top fibers are in tension and the bottom fibers are in compression. When the top fibers are in compression and bottom fibers are in tension, the bending moment is positive.

The answer is C.

10. The bending moment in a beam is maximum when the shear is

A. maximum
B. equal to zero
C. minimum
D. at its greatest absolute value

Solution

Shear (V) is the derivative of the bending moment (M).

$$V = \frac{dM}{dx}$$

According to the principles of calculus, the bending moment reaches its maximum value when its derivative (the shear) is zero. All the other statements are false.

The answer is B.

11. What are the support reactions (R_A and R_B) for the beam loaded as shown?

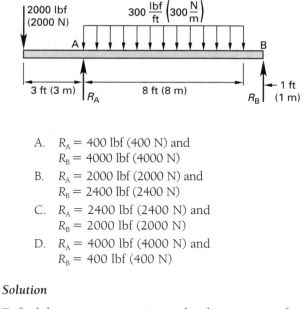

A. $R_A = 400$ lbf (400 N) and
$R_B = 4000$ lbf (4000 N)

B. $R_A = 2000$ lbf (2000 N) and
$R_B = 2400$ lbf (2400 N)

C. $R_A = 2400$ lbf (2400 N) and
$R_B = 2000$ lbf (2000 N)

D. $R_A = 4000$ lbf (4000 N) and
$R_B = 400$ lbf (400 N)

Solution

To find these support reactions, solve the equations of equilibrium for the beam. The sum of all moments equals zero, and the sum of all vertical forces equals zero.

$$\Sigma M = 0$$

$$\Sigma F_y = 0$$

The sum of the moments can be calculated either about support A or about support B. The uniformly distributed load is replaced by its resultant (R) acting at the center of the load 4 ft (4 m) from support A.

$$R = (300)(8) = 2400$$

Taking moments about support A, with clockwise being positive,

$$\Sigma M_A = 0$$
$$-(2000)(3) + (2400)(4) - R_B(9) = 0$$
$$R_B = 400$$

Balancing forces,

$$\Sigma F_y = 0$$
$$2000 - R_A + 2400 - 400 = 0$$
$$R_A = 4000$$

The answer is D.

12. The correct shear diagram for the beam loaded as shown is

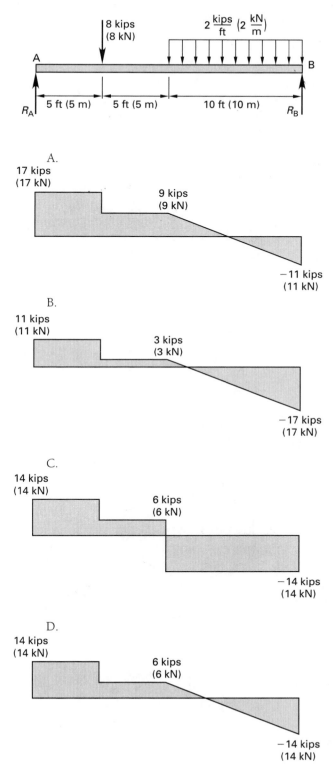

Solution

Calculate the support reactions of the beam by solving the equations of equilibrium.

$$\Sigma M = 0$$

$$\Sigma F_y = 0$$

The sum of moments can be calculated either about support A or about support B. The uniform load is replaced by its resultant (R), which is considered to act at the center of the load 5 ft (5 m) from support B.

$$R = (2)(10) = 20$$

Calculating the sum of moments at support B, with clockwise being positve,

$$\Sigma M_B = 0$$

$$R_A(20) - (8)(15) - (20)(5) = 0$$

$$R_A = 11$$

Balancing forces,

$$\Sigma F_y = 0$$

$$11 - 8 - 20 + R_B = 0$$

$$R_B = 17$$

The answer is B.

TRUSS ANALYSIS

13.   What are the forces (F_1 and F_2, respectively) in mem-

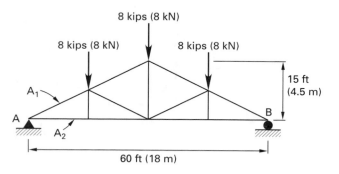

8 kips (8 kN)

8 kips (8 kN)   8 kips (8 kN)

15 ft
(4.5 m)

A_1

A   B

A_2

60 ft (18 m)

bers A_1 and A_2 of the truss shown?

    A. $F_1 = 12$ kips (12 kN) in compression
        $F_2 = 12$ kips (12 kN) in tension
    B. $F_1 = 12$ kips (12 kN) in tension
        $F_2 = 12$ kips (12 kN) in compression
    C. $F_1 = 27$ kips (27 kN) in compression
        $F_2 = 24$ kips (24 kN) in tension
    D. $F_1 = 27$ kips (27 kN) in tension
        $F_2 = 24$ kips (24 kN) in compression

Solution

To find the forces in members A_1 and A_1, first find the support reactions of the truss.

The truss and the loading are symmetrical, so the support reactions (R_A and R_B) are equal and each one is one-half of the total load on the truss.

$$R_A = R_B = \frac{(8)(3)}{2} = 12$$

Next, apply the *method of joints* (or analysis by joint equilibrium) in truss analysis and analyze joint A at the left end support. Draw a free-body diagram for joint A, then solve the two equations of equilibrium.

$$\Sigma F_x = 0$$

$$\Sigma F_y = 0$$

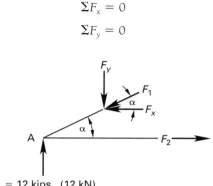

$R_A = 12$ kips   (12 kN)

$$\Sigma F_y = 0$$

$$12 - F_y = 0$$

$$F_y = 12$$

$$= F_1 \sin \alpha$$

$$F_1 = \frac{F_y}{\sin \alpha} = \frac{12}{\sin \alpha}$$

Find α from the dimensions of the large triangle that is the left half of the truss.

In U.S. units:

$$\tan \alpha = \frac{15 \text{ ft}}{30 \text{ ft}} = 0.5$$

$$\alpha = 26.6°$$

In SI units:

$$\tan \alpha = \frac{4.5 \text{ m}}{9 \text{ m}} = 0.5$$

$$\alpha = 26.6°$$

Substituting the value of α into the equation for F_1,

$$F_1 = \frac{F_y}{\sin \alpha} = \frac{12}{\sin 26.6°} = \frac{12}{0.448}$$

$$= 26.8 \quad (27 \text{ compression})$$

$$\Sigma F_x = 0$$

$$F_2 - F_x = 0$$

$$F_x = F_1 \cos \alpha = (26.8)(\cos 26.6°)$$

$$= 23.96 \quad (24 \text{ compression})$$

The force in a member of a truss is a *compression force* when it points toward the joint being analyzed (joint A in this case), and it is a *tension force* when it is pulling away from the analyzed joint.

The answer is C.

WOOD STRUCTURES AND STRUCTURAL SYSTEMS

14. Glulam members of the stress class 24F have an allowable bending stress of

    A. 24 psi
    B. 240 psi
    C. 2400 psi
    D. 24,000 psi

Solution

For glulam members of the stress class 24F, the allowable bending stress (F_b) is 2400 psi. The number preceding the letter F in the combination symbol of glulam is always the value of F_b in hundreds of psi.

The answer is C.

15. Wood I-joists are generally spaced

    A. at 5 ft (1.5 m) o.c.
    B. at 10 ft (3 m) o.c.
    C. like lumber joists, often at 12 in (305), 16 in (406), or 24 in (610) o.c.
    D. at any desired spacing

Solution

I-joists are normally spaced like lumber joists. Load-span design tables include spacing values of 12 in (305), 16 in (406), 19.2 in (488), and 24 in (610) on center.

Wood I-joists function like steel I-beams. The flanges are generally made of lumber or laminated veneer lumber and resist most of the bending stress. The web is often made of plywood or OSB (oriented strand board) and resists most of the shear. I-joists are standardized under the designation APA Performance Rated I-Joist (PRI) by APA, The Engineered Wood Association.

The answer is C.

16. In wood-framed buildings, the thickness of the plywood subfloor is

    A. dependent on the sizes of supporting joists
    B. dependent on the spacing of supporting joists
    C. not related to the supporting joists
    D. always $\frac{1}{2}$ in (13)

Solution

Traditional floor systems consist of the subfloor, sometimes an underlayment, and a finish floor. Subfloors are now built with structural wood panels made of plywood, oriented strand board, oriented wafer board, or composite plywood (comply). The thickness is most often between $\frac{3}{8}$ in (9.5) and $1\frac{1}{8}$ in (28.5). Subfloor thickness does not need to be calculated because it is specified based on the maximum joist spacing.

The answer is B.

17. Which of the following statements about sawn lumber joists in wood-framed buildings are true? (Choose the four that apply.)

    A. Joists often have a nominal width of 2 in (51).
    B. Joists often have a nominal depth of 6 in (152) to 28 in (711).
    C. For heavy loads, joists may have a nominal width of 3 in (76) to 4 in (102).
    D. Double joists must be provided under partitions parallel to the joists.
    E. Joists are often spaced at 12 in (305) or 16 in (406) o.c.
    F. Joists rarely span more than 10 ft (3.0 m).

Solution

Statements B and F are both false. Lumber joists often have nominal depths of 6 in (152) to 14 in (356). The depth of 28 in (711) is not included in the table of standard sizes for sawn lumber joists. Statement B is therefore false. Statement F is false because lumber joists often span 15 ft to 20 ft (4.6 m to 6.1 m), and sometimes more.

The answer is A, C, D, and E.

18.   In the floor framing of wood-framed buildings using lumber joists, rows of bridging are generally provided

I.   at the joist midspan
II.   on rows spaced 4 ft (1.2 m) apart
III.   on rows not more than 8 ft (2.4 m) apart
IV.   in the form of cross bridging or solid blocking

    A.   I and II only
    B.   III and IV only
    C.   I, II, and IV only
    D.   I, III, and IV only

Solution

The true statements are I, III, and IV. In the floor framing of wood-framed buildings, bridging is normally provided in the form of cross bridging or solid blocking at the joist midspan, and on rows not more than 8 ft (2.4 m) apart. The function of the bridging is to distribute the concentrated loads over several joists, which increases the strength of the floor and the resistance to lateral loads.

There are two types of bridging: cross bridging and solid blocking. Solid blocking is generally preferred, and consists of short pieces of wood (the same size as the joists) fitted perpendicular to and between the joists. Cross bridging or X-bracing (usually 1×2 lumber) is placed diagonally between the joists and is nailed in at the top and bottom.

The answer is D.

19.   Dimension lumber elements have a nominal width of

    A.   less than 2 in (51)
    B.   2 in (51) to 4 in (102)
    C.   4 in (102) to 6 in (152)
    D.   more than 5 in (127)

Solution

Sawn lumber elements are generally classified into three categories: elements with a nominal thickness of less than 2 in (51) are *boards*; elements with a nominal width between 2 in (51) and 4 in (102) are *dimension lumber*; and elements with a thickness of more than 5 in (127) are *timbers*. There is no classification of elements with a nominal width between 4 in (102) and 6 in (152).

The answer is B.

20.   Which of the following statements about heavy timber construction is NOT true?

    A.   Heavy timber construction is sometimes called slow-burning or mill construction.
    B.   Heavy timber construction requires exterior walls of noncombustible materials, such as masonry or concrete.
    C.   The minimum size of columns in heavy timber construction is 4 in (102) by 4 in (102).
    D.   The fire resistance in heavy timber construction is mainly due to the large size of the structural elements, which burn slowly.

Solution

All statements are true except C. Building codes identify the minimum size of columns in heavy timber construction as 8 in (203) by 8 in (203), not 4 in (102) by 4 in (102).

The answer is C.

21.   Which of the following effects could be attributed to longitudinal shrinkage of members in wood-framed buildings?

I.   unequal vertical movements at different points
II.   cracking of plaster
III.   cracking of glass
IV.   opening up of joints

    A.   I and IV only
    B.   I, II, and III only
    C.   II, III, and IV only
    D.   I, II, III, and IV

Solution

All the listed effects could be due to longitudinal shrinkage of wood framing members. The longitudinal shrinkage of wood is generally negligible. The cross-grain shrinkage is relatively large when there is a reduction in moisture content. Vertical shrinkage produces unequal vertical movements at different points, leading to problems such as cracking of plaster and glass, and opening up of joints.

Balloon framing has a smaller amount of longitudinal shrinkage compared to platform framing. This is due to the continuity of the wall studs through the full height of the building. Platform framing produces considerable cross-grain shrinkage along the lines of vertical support. Platform framing is, however, used more frequently due to its ease of construction.

The answer is D.

22.   Which of the following statements about glued laminated timber (glulam) are true? (Choose the four that apply.)

    A.   Glulam is fabricated from thin layers of wood glued together.

    B.   Glulam generally consists of 2 to 60 lams.

    C.   Both dry-use adhesives and watertight glue can be used to fabricate glulam.

    D.   Glulam girders span no more than 60 ft (18.3 m).

    E.   Standard widths of glulam beams are roughly between 2 in (51) and 14 in (356).

    F.   The usual thickness of each lam is about 6 in (152).

Solution

The false statements are D and F. Statement D is false because glulam girders with spans exceeding 100 ft (30.5 m) have been constructed. Statement F is false because the lam (or layer) thickness of glulam is standardized, generally between 1^1/$_2$ in (38) and 2 in (51) nominal. ^{3}/$_4$ in (19) lams are generally used for curved beams because they are easier to bend.

Sawn lumber elements are limited in size by the size of the trees they come from. Glulam elements, however, can be of longer sizes and spans than sawn lumber. This is possible because they are fabricated from thin laminations of wood glued together. The number of laminations is generally between 2 and 60. The standard beam widths are roughly between 2 in (51) and 14 in (356). Lam thicknesses are standardized as explained above. A dry-use adhesive is used for interior glulam elements, and a wet-use adhesive (watertight glue) is used for elements to be used outdoors or in a humid environment.

The answer is A, B, C, and E.

23.   A simply supported glulam beam spanning 48 ft carries the following loads: 200 lbf/ft of dead load and 1000 lbf/ft of floor live load. The glulam is 24F-V5 DF/HF—Western Species. Assume dry conditions, normal temperature, and a volume factor of 0.9. The minimum required section modulus for this beam is _____ in^3. (Fill in the blank.)

Solution

The minimum required section modulus is

$$S_{req} = \frac{M_{max}}{F'_b}$$

M_{max} is the maximum bending moment. F'_b is the modified or adjusted allowable bending stress.

The total of the dead and live loads is

$$w = 200 \, \frac{lbf}{ft} + 1000 \, \frac{lbf}{ft} = 1200 \, lbf/ft$$

The maximum bending moment for a simply supported beam loaded with a uniformly distributed load is

$$M_{max} = \frac{wL^2}{8}$$

$$= \frac{\left(1200 \, \dfrac{lbf}{ft}\right)(48 \, ft)^2}{8} = 345{,}600 \, \text{ft-lbf}$$

The modified or adjusted allowable bending stress is obtained by multiplying the reference allowable bending stress by the different applicable adjustment factors. For a 24F-glulam, the allowable bending stress is 2400 psi. The wet service factor (C_M) is 1 for dry conditions. The temperature factor (C_t) is 1 for normal temperature. The load duration factor (C_D) is 1 for floor live load, and the volume factor (C_v) is given as 0.9.

$$F'_b = F_b C_M C_t C_D C_v$$

$$= \left(2400 \, \frac{lbf}{in^2}\right)(1)(1)(1)(0.9) = 2160 \, lbf/in^2$$

$$S_{req} = \frac{M_{max}}{F'_b}$$

$$= \frac{(345{,}600 \, \text{ft-lbf})\left(12 \, \dfrac{in}{ft}\right)}{2160 \, \dfrac{lbf}{in^2}} = 1920 \, in^3$$

The answer is 1920 in^3.

24. A sawn lumber roof joist is simply supported over a span of 14 ft. There is a roof dead load of 14 psf and a roof live load of 20 psf. Joists are spaced at 16 in on center. Plywood roof sheathing prevents lateral buckling. The material is no. 1 hem-fir. Assume dry conditions and a normal temperature. For no. 1 hem-fir, the allowable bending stress is 975 psi. Use Table 1, Section Properties of Standard Dressed (S4S) Sawn Lumber, in the Appendix. The size factor is

$$C_F = 1.3 \text{ for } 2 \times 6$$
$$C_F = 1.2 \text{ for } 2 \times 8$$
$$C_F = 1.1 \text{ for } 2 \times 10$$

The required size for this joist in bending is 2 × ____. (Fill in the blank.)

Solution

The minimum required section modulus is

$$S_{req} = \frac{M_{max}}{F'_b}$$

M_{max} is the maximum bending moment. F'_b is the modified or adjusted allowable bending stress.

The linear loads per foot are calculated by multiplying the uniform load per square foot times the tributary width, which is the spacing between joists spaced 16 in on center, or 1.33 ft.

$$w_{total} = \left(14 \frac{\text{lbf}}{\text{ft}^2} + 20 \frac{\text{lbf}}{\text{ft}^2}\right)(1.33 \text{ ft}) = 45.33 \text{ lbf/ft}$$

The maximum bending moment for a simply supported beam loaded with a uniformly distributed load is

$$M_{max} = \frac{wL^2}{8}$$

$$= \frac{\left(45.33 \frac{\text{lbf}}{\text{ft}}\right)(14 \text{ ft})^2}{8} = 1110.6 \text{ ft-lbf}$$

The modified or adjusted allowable bending stress is obtained by multiplying the reference allowable bending stress of 975 psi by the different applicable adjustment factors. The wet service factor (C_M) is 1 for dry conditions. The temperature factor (C_t) is 1 for normal temperature. The load duration factor (C_D) is 1.25 for roof live load, and the size factor (C_F) is assumed and adjusted later. The repetitive member factor (C_r) is 1.15; it applies here because parallel

dimension lumber joists are used and are spaced at less than 24 in on center. Assuming a size factor (C_F) of 1.3,

$$F'_b = F_b C_M C_t C_D C_F C_r$$

$$= \left(975 \frac{\text{lbf}}{\text{in}^2}\right)(1)(1)(1.25)(1.3)(1.15) = 1822 \text{ lbf/in}^2$$

$$S_{req} = \frac{M_{max}}{F'_b}$$

$$= \frac{(1110.6 \text{ ft-lbf})\left(12 \frac{\text{in}}{\text{ft}}\right)}{1822 \frac{\text{lbf}}{\text{in}^2}} = 7.31 \text{ in}^3$$

Using Table 1 in the Appendix, select the smallest size with a section modulus (S_{xx}) of at least 7.31 in³. This is 2×6 with a section modulus of 7.563 in³. The size factor is then checked. This factor is given in the table as 1.3 for 2×6, as assumed.

The answer is 2×6.

STEEL STRUCTURES AND STRUCTURAL SYSTEMS

25. To support the roof of a building with an extra-long span, the most economical steel structural system is

    A.   trusses
    B.   arches
    C.   rigid frames
    D.   steel cables

Solution

For the roof of a building with an extra-long span, the most economical steel structural system is a cable system. The cost of roof support per square foot using cables is generally lower than the cost of using other rigid steel structural systems.

It is estimated that based on normal allowable working stresses and a 10% sag for a suspended cable, a 36 in (914) W-shaped beam can carry its own weight for about 220 ft (67 m), while a steel cable can carry its own weight for about 3.3 mi (5.3 km).

The answer is D.

26. The structural steel shape W12×26 has an approximate depth and linear weight, respectively, of

    A. 12 in and 26 lbf/ft
    B. 26 in and 12 lbf/ft
    C. 12 in and 12 lbf/ft
    D. 26 in and 26 lbf/ft

Solution

A W12×26 is a wide-flange structural I-shaped steel beam with a depth of approximately 12 in and a linear weight of 26 lbf/ft. The first number following the letter W in the designation is always the approximate depth, and the second number is always the weight in pounds per foot.

The answer is A.

27. What are the most frequently used steel rolled beam shapes?

    A. structural tees
    B. angles, or L shapes
    C. W shapes
    D. M shapes

Solution

The most frequently used steel rolled beam shapes are the W shapes, which are I-sections with wide parallel flanges. Structural tees and angles are generally used in applications other than beams, such as lintels and truss members. M shapes are miscellaneous shapes with an I-section. They are generally lightweight and available from a number of producers or, infrequently, rolled. Though they are occasionally used as beams, this is not as common as the W shapes.

The answer is C.

28. Which steel beams are most susceptible to lateral buckling?

    A. beams that have wide shallow sections
    B. beams that have deep narrow sections
    C. beams that have square sections
    D. all beam sections are equally susceptible

Solution

The tendency of a beam to buckle increases relative to the ratio I_x/I_y, where I_x is the moment of inertia about the horizontal centroidal axis and I_y is the moment of inertia about the vertical centroidal axis.

This ratio is larger in deep, narrow sections. The answer is therefore B. Choice D is incorrect since all sections are not equally susceptible to buckling. The I_x/I_y ratio is smaller in wide, shallow sections and square sections, so choices A and C are incorrect. It should also be noted that square sections are generally not used in beams.

The answer is B.

29. A steel beam is simply supported over a span of 20 ft and carries a total design point load of 6 kips at the center of the span. The moment of inertia (I_x) for this beam is 245 in⁴. Neglecting the beam weight, the maximum total load deflection of this beam is _____ in. (Fill in the blank.)

Solution

For a simply supported beam with a point load at the center of the span, the maximum deflection is at midspan and is

$$\Delta_{max} = \frac{PL^3}{48EI}$$

P is the point load, L is the length of the span, E is the modulus of elasticity (for steel, $E = 29{,}000$ ksi), and I is the moment of inertia about the bending axis (here the x-x axis).

Substituting,

$$\Delta_{max} = \frac{(6 \text{ kips})(20 \text{ ft})^3 \left(12 \frac{\text{in}}{\text{ft}}\right)^3}{(48)\left(29{,}000 \frac{\text{kips}}{\text{in}^2}\right)(245 \text{ in}^4)} = 0.24 \text{ in}$$

The answer is 0.24 in.

30. For short spans and in relatively small openings in 8 in (203) and 12 in (305) thick brick walls, the most commonly used steel lintels are

    A. angles placed back to back
    B. channels or C shapes
    C. W shapes used for beams
    D. structural T shapes

Solution

In short spans and relatively small openings in 8 in (203) and 12 in (305) thick brick walls, the most commonly used steel lintels are angles placed back to back. Three steel angles are sometimes used. The W shape beam is often used for longer spans or thicker walls.

The answer is A.

31. Open-web K-series steel joists can span up to

A. 40 ft (12 m)
B. 60 ft (18 m)
C. 80 ft (24 m)
D. 100 ft (30.5 m)

Solution

Open-web K-series steel joists can span up to 60 ft (18 m). The depth range for the K-series joists is from 8 in (203) to 30 in (762), in 2 in (51) increments.

The answer is B.

32. Which of the following statements about bridging of open-web joists is FALSE?

A. Bridging must be provided for lateral stability
B. Bridging provides stability mainly to the upper chords of joists.
C. Bridging may be horizontal or diagonal.
D. The size of bridging required depends on the slenderness ratio of the element.

Solution

The false statement is B. Bridging provides lateral stability mainly to lower chords, not upper chords. Upper chords are held in place by the decking material.

All other statements about bridging are true. Bridging may be horizontal or diagonal. The purpose of using bridging is to provide lateral stability. However, there is a second purpose as well for the diagonal bridging and that is to transfer a portion of any concentrated load or localized overload to the adjacent joist. Horizontal bridging will not do that.

The size of bridging depends on the slenderness ratio (L/r) of the unbraced length to the least radius of gyration. For horizontal bridging, the requirement is a ratio of less than or equal to 300. For diagonal bridging, the requirement is a ratio of less than or equal to 200. Angles and L shapes are often used for bridging.

The answer is B.

33. For spans of 300 ft (91 m) or more, the most appropriate steel structural system is generally

A. a skeleton frame comprised of beams, girders, and columns
B. steel trusses
C. steel rigid frames
D. steel arches

Solution

For spans of 300 ft (91 m) or more, the most appropriate steel structural system is generally steel arches. Steel arches are used extensively to support roofs covering large unobstructed floor areas in structures such as hangars, field houses, and exhibition halls with spans often exceeding 300 ft (91 m). Rigid frames are generally preferred for intermediate spans.

The answer is D.

34. The components of a steel rigid frame are generally

I.   steel channels
II.   steel tubes
III. wide-flange shapes
IV. built-up sections from a web plate to which flange plates are fillet welded

A. I and II only
B. I and III only
C. III and IV only
D. II, III, and IV only

Solution

The correct options are III and IV. Rigid frame components may be wide-flange shapes (W shapes) or they could be built up of a web plate to which flange plates are fillet welded.

The answer is C.

35. Which of the following statements are true about the use of stiffeners in steel rigid frames? (Choose the three that apply.)

    A. Stiffeners consist of steel plates fitted between the flanges.

    B. Stiffeners are generally bolted to the flanges and web.

    C. Stiffeners are generally used only where point loads are applied.

    D. Stiffeners are used to help prevent the buckling of flanges.

    E. Stiffeners are used in various locations, including at the crown and at points of change in direction.

    F. Stiffeners are generally used only at the center of each knee.

Solution

A stiffener is a plate used to increase the capacity of a member's web and flanges to resist buckling. The stiffener fits between the flanges, normal to the web, and is welded to the web and flanges. Stiffeners are used to reinforce members at various locations, such as load points, bearing points, points of directional change, and at ends of frame sections at the crown and the center of each knee. Statements B, C, and E are, therefore, false.

The answer is A, D, and F.

36. Which statement is FALSE?

    A. The most common type of steel arch is the three-hinged arch.

    B. In a three-hinged arch, the horizontal movement of the abutments due to outward thrusts cannot be prevented.

    C. Steel arches can be trussed.

    D. Steel arches can be used with spans exceeding 300 ft (91 m).

Solution

The false statement is choice B, because in a three-hinged arch the horizontal movement of the abutments due to outward thrusts can be prevented simply by tying the two abutments together with tie rods. All other statements about steel arches are true.

The answer is B.

37. A W10×30 rolled steel shape of ASTM A242 grade 50 steel is used as a simply supported beam over a span of 20 ft. The beam carries a uniformly distributed load of 2.4 kips/ft over its entire span, including an allowance for its self-weight. The section modulus of the W10×30 is 32.4 in³. The allowable bending stress is 0.66F_y. The maximum resisting moment of this beam is about

    A. 64 ft-kips
    B. 89 ft-kips
    C. 950 ft-kips
    D. 1100 ft-kips

Solution

The maximum resisting moment (M_R) is the maximum moment capacity of a beam section, and is

$$M_R = F_b S_x$$

The allowable bending stress (F_b) is calculated using the equation provided in the problem. The yield stress (F_y) of the ASTM A242 grade 50 steel is 50 ksi.

$$F_b = 0.66F_y$$

$$= (0.66)\left(50 \ \frac{\text{kips}}{\text{in}^2}\right)$$

$$= 33 \ \text{ksi}$$

$$M_R = F_b S_x = \frac{\left(33 \ \dfrac{\text{kips}}{\text{in}^2}\right)(32.4 \ \text{in}^3)}{12 \ \dfrac{\text{in}}{\text{ft}}}$$

$$= 89.1 \ \text{ft-kips} \quad (89 \ \text{ft-kips})$$

The answer is B.

38. An S10×35 rolled steel shape of ASTM A588 grade 50 steel is used as cantilever beam over a span of 8 ft. The beam carries 1500 lbf/ft over its entire span, including its own weight. The S10×35 has a web thickness of ⁵⁄₈ in (or 0.594 in). The maximum average unit shear stress in this beam according to the AISC Specification is about

    A. 1000 psi
    B. 2000 psi
    C. 6000 psi
    D. 12,000 psi

Solution

The AISC Specification provides the following equation to calculate the maximum average unit shear stress in a steel beam.

$$f_v = \frac{V_{max}}{A_w}$$

The maximum shear force (V_{max}) in the beam is equal to the largest support reaction. In this case, the beam is cantilevered and has only one reaction (R). This reaction must equal the total load on the beam, which can be obtained by multiplying the uniformly distributed load (w) by the length of the span (L).

$$
\begin{aligned}
V_{max} &= R = wL \\
&= \left(1500 \, \frac{lbf}{ft}\right)(8 \, ft) \\
&= 12{,}000 \, lbf
\end{aligned}
$$

The web area of the beam section (A_w) is

$$A_w = dt_w$$

d is the beam depth. For an S10-section, the depth is 10 in. t_w is the thickness of the web, which is given as $5/8$ in (or 0.594 in).

$$
\begin{aligned}
A_w &= dt_w \\
&= (10 \, in)(0.594 \, in) \\
&= 5.94 \, in^2 \\
f_v &= \frac{V_{max}}{A_w} \\
&= \frac{12{,}000 \, lbf}{5.94 \, in^2} \\
&= 2020 \, lbf/in^2 \quad (2000 \, psi)
\end{aligned}
$$

The answer is B.

CONCRETE STRUCTURES AND STRUCTURAL SYSTEMS

39.   Columns of a seven-story building are located on a square grid, 20 ft by 20 ft (6 m by 6 m). Service loads at each level are 90 psf (4.3 kN/m²) of dead load and 50 psf (2.4 kN/m²) of live load, including self-weights. What is the approximate total axial load on a typical first-floor interior column?

    A.   75 kips (320 kN)
    B.   390 kips (1700 kN)
    C.   450 kips (1900 kN)
    D.   530 kips (2300 kN)

Solution

Based on the ACI code, *service loads*, which are the real expected loads, must be multiplied by *load factors* (safety factors). The resulting loads, called *ultimate loads*, are used in design. Dead loads are multiplied by a factor of 1.2, and live loads are multiplied by a factor of 1.6. The total ultimate load is then multiplied by the tributary area of an interior column, which here is 20 ft by 20 ft (6 m by 6 m), and by the number of levels above that column, in this case seven. The ultimate uniform load is

$$W_u = 1.2W_{DL} + 1.6W_{LL}$$

In U.S. units:

$$W_u = (1.2)\left(90 \, \frac{lbf}{ft^2}\right) + (1.6)\left(50 \, \frac{lbf}{ft^2}\right) = 188 \, lbf/ft^2$$

$$P_{total} = \left(188 \, \frac{lbf}{ft^2}\right)(400 \, ft^2)(7) = 526{,}400 \, lbf \quad (530 \, kips)$$

In SI units:

$$W_u = (1.2)\left(4.3 \, \frac{kN}{m^2}\right) + (1.6)\left(2.4 \, \frac{kN}{m^2}\right) = 9.0 \, kN/m^2$$

$$P_{total} = \left(9.0 \, \frac{kN}{m^2}\right)(36 \, m^2)(7) = 2268 \, kN \quad (2300 \, kN)$$

The answer is D.

40. Which of following statements about reinforcing bars is FALSE?

    A. Reinforcing bars used as main reinforcement for moment are generally deformed bars.

    B. Bar sizes are designated by numbers that generally represent the number of eighths of an inch in the nominal diameter.

    C. Today, only grades 40 and 60 steel are used in making rebar in building construction.

    D. In grade 40 and 60 steel, the numbers refer to the steel's yield strength in ksi.

Solution

Option C is the false statement. There are three strengths of steel used in making rebar today: grades 40, 60, and 75, representing steels with yield strengths of 40 ksi, 60 ksi, and 75 ksi, respectively. Grade 40 was once very common, but now it is generally found in only the smallest rebar sizes, such as #3 and #4 rebar. Grade 75 is the highest strength steel grade and is seldom used.

The answer is C.

41. A reinforced concrete slab is generally considered a one-way slab when the ratio of long span to short span is

    A. 1.0

    B. 2.0 or more

    C. 3.0 or more

    D. 4.0 or more

Solution

A reinforced concrete slab is generally considered a one-way slab when the ratio of long span to short span is 2.0 or more, and it is considered a two-way slab when the ratio is less than 2.0. A one-way slab is reinforced for bending moment in the short direction, and for temperature and shrinkage stresses at the minimum ratio in the long direction. A two-way slab is reinforced for bending moment in both directions.

The answer is B.

42. A pan joist concrete deck system is a

    A. concrete slab ribbed in both directions

    B. concrete slab ribbed in one direction only

    C. flat slab supported on columns with shearheads

    D. flat slab supported on beams

Solution

A *pan joist concrete deck system* is a reinforced concrete slab ribbed in one direction only. The ribs are usually 18 in (457) to 30 in (762) on center. The joists generally run in the short direction, and the beams in the long direction. For visual reasons, the system is seldom exposed. It is usually used for heavier loads such as storage or industrial buildings.

A concrete slab ribbed in both directions is called a *waffle slab*.

The answer is B.

43. A building is being planned for the storage of industrial equipment and machinery. What is the most appropriate reinforced concrete slab system for this building?

    A. a flat slab on columns

    B. a flat slab on columns equipped with shearheads

    C. a flat slab on beams on all four sides

    D. a pan joist concrete deck system

Solution

The most appropriate reinforced concrete slab system for this building is a pan joist system. A flat slab on columns is generally used for light loads such as in residential buildings. Adding shearheads or beams on all four sides of the flat slab resolves the punching shear problem around the columns, and allows the system to be used for slightly longer spans and heavier loads, but would still be insufficient for storing industrial equipment and machinery. A pan joist system is the strongest system of the options listed, and it is the best suited for the heavy live loads of industrial and storage buildings.

The answer is D.

44.   What is the approximate span limit for a reinforced concrete waffle slab with no prestressing?

    A.   20 ft (6 m)
    B.   30 ft to 35 ft (9 m to 11 m)
    C.   40 ft to 50 ft (12 m to 15 m)
    D.   80 ft to 90 ft (24 m to 27 m)

Solution

The span limit for a reinforced concrete waffle slab without prestressing is approximately 40 ft (12 m) to 50 ft (15 m). The waffle slab constitutes a relatively strong concrete deck system. When prestressed, this slab could span up to 80 ft (24 m) or more.

The answer is C.

45.   In general, the most commonly used reinforced concrete slab system is the

    A.   waffle slab
    B.   flat slab on beams
    C.   one-way slab
    D.   pan joist system

Solution

The most commonly used reinforced concrete slab system is the one-way slab, because beams in this system can be placed on an irregular column grid. The slab forms a rectangle with the main reinforcement running parallel to the short direction. Only a minimum amount of reinforcement, to resist temperature and shrinkage stresses, is placed in the long direction.

The answer is C.

46.   In a one-way reinforced concrete slab, typical short direction spans are

I.   10 ft and 12 ft (3.0 m and 3.7 m)
II.   14 ft and 16 ft (4.3 m and 4.9 m)
III. 18 ft and 20 ft (5.5 m and 6.1 m)
IV. 22 ft and 24 ft (6.7 m and 7.3 m)

    A.   IV only
    B.   I and II only
    C.   II and III only
    D.   II, III, and IV only

Solution

In a one-way reinforced concrete slab, typical short direction spans are: 10, 12, 14, and 16 ft (3.0, 3.7, 4.3, and 4.9 m).

The answer is B.

47.   What is the general function of the main rebars in reinforced concrete?

    A.   to resist tension
    B.   to resist compression
    C.   to resist torsion
    D.   all of the above

Solution

The general function of the main rebars in reinforced concrete is to resist the tension stresses (choice A). Reinforced concrete is a composite material made of concrete and reinforcing bars. Concrete generally resists the compression stresses, and the reinforcing steel generally resists the tension stresses that concrete cannot resist. Concrete cracks easily under tension, so the tensile strength of concrete is generally neglected in the design. In rare cases, rebars can be placed in the compression zone to help concrete resist some of the compression stresses. In this case, the reinforcement is referred to as *compression reinforcement*. However, instead of using compression reinforcement, engineers normally increase the concrete section of the beam if possible.

The answer is A.

48.   The reinforcing bars in a cantilevered beam or slab are generally placed

    A.   at the bottom
    B.   at the top
    C.   at either the top or the bottom depending on the location of the beam or slab in a building
    D.   at either the top or the bottom depending on the value of the maximum bending moment

Solution

In a cantilevered beam or slab, the bending moment is negative, which means that the top fibers are stressed in tension and the bottom fibers are stressed in compression. Since the function of the reinforcing steel is to resist tension, rebars must be placed in the top (choice B).

Choice C is incorrect because the location of a cantilevered beam or slab in a building has nothing to do with its bending moment. The bending moment is always negative in the cantilever when it is subjected to gravity loads, which is most often the case. Choice D is incorrect because it is the type and not the value of the bending moment that determines the location of the rebars. For a positive bending moment, the rebars are at the bottom; for a negative bending moment, the rebars are at the top, which is the case in the cantilever.

The answer is B.

49. A reinforced concrete column can be either laterally or spirally tied. Which of these types of columns is generally spirally tied?

    A. square
    B. rectangular
    C. circular
    D. T-shaped

Solution

Reinforced concrete columns with a circular or octagonal cross sections are generally spirally tied. Square and rectangular columns are usually laterally tied.

With spirally tied columns, a $^3/_8$ in (9.5) or $^1/_2$ in (13) smooth wire is generally used with a minimum spacing of 1 in (25) and a maximum spacing of 3 in (76).

Laterally tied columns cost less than spirally tied ones and are used more often. However, spirally tied columns are tougher and perform better under seismic loads.

The answer is C.

50. According to ACI code requirements, the minimum thickness for a one-way simply supported reinforced concrete slab with a span L is

    A. $L/10$
    B. $L/20$
    C. $L/28$
    D. $L/40$

Solution

According to ACI 318, Table 9.5(a), the minimum thickness for a one-way simply supported reinforced concrete slab with a span L is $L/20$. $L/10$ is the minimum thickness for a cantilevered slab, and $L/28$ is the minimum thickness for a continuous one-way slab. Option D, $L/40$, does not represent any of the ACI code requirements.

The answer is B.

51. According to the ACI code requirements, a cantilevered reinforced concrete slab spanning 10 ft (3.05 m) needs to have a minimum thickness of

    A. 6 in (152)
    B. 12 in (305)
    C. 20 in (508)
    D. 24 in (610)

Solution

According to ACI 318, Table 9.5(a), a cantilevered reinforced concrete slab of a span L needs to have a minimum thickness of $L/10$.

In U.S. units:

$$h = \frac{L}{10} = \frac{(10 \text{ ft})\left(12 \frac{\text{in}}{\text{ft}}\right)}{10}$$

$$= 12 \text{ in}$$

In SI units:

$$h = \frac{L}{10} = \frac{(3.05 \text{ m})\left(1000 \frac{\text{mm}}{\text{m}}\right)}{10}$$

$$= 305 \text{ mm}$$

The answer is B.

52. Aggregates generally represent what percentage of concrete volume?

    A. 20% to 30%
    B. 35% to 45%
    C. 60% to 75%
    D. 80% to 85%

Solution

Aggregates generally represent 60% to 75% of concrete volume. Aggregates are classified as fine or coarse. Fine aggregates, like sand, can pass through a $^3/_8$ in (9.5) sieve; coarse aggregates are larger. The quality of aggregates is very important, since they represent a large percentage of the concrete volume. Well-graded aggregates reduce the amount of cement paste needed and help make the concrete mix more workable.

The answer is C.

53. What are the most frequently used types of portland cement?

I.   Type I (general purpose)
II. Type II (sulfate resisting)
III. Type III (high early strength)
IV. Type IV (low heat of hydration)

    A.   I and II only
    B.   I and III only
    C.   I, III, and IV only
    D.   II, III, and IV only

Solution

The most frequently used types of portland cement are Type I (general purpose) and Type III (high early strength). Type I is the least expensive and it is used in general applications. Type III is used when high strength is needed at an early age. High-early-strength concrete allows forms to be removed sooner and reused quickly, thus reducing construction time.

Type IV is no longer produced. The same benefits of low heat of hydration are now achieved with the addition of fly ash or slag to the mix. Type II, sulfate-resisting cement, is used only when the structure is in contact with either soil or water containing sulfate.

The answer is B.

54. What is the balanced steel ratio as applied to reinforced concrete?

    A.   the maximum steel reinforcement ratio
    B.   the minimum steel reinforcement ratio for stresses due to temperature or shrinkage
    C.   the steel reinforcement ratio that would result in a simultaneous yielding of the steel and crushing of the concrete
    D.   one-half of the maximum steel reinforcement ratio

Solution

The balanced steel ratio is the reinforcement ratio that would result in a simultaneous yielding of the steel and crushing of the concrete. The maximum reinforcement ratio mandated by the ACI code is 75% of the balanced steel ratio. For preliminary design purposes, the reinforcement ratio is generally kept in the range of 40% to 60% of the balanced ratio. This generally results in economical beam sizes.

The answer is C.

55. In residential applications, the minimum thickness for a concrete slab on grade is generally

    A.   1 in (25)
    B.   4 in (102)
    C.   8 in (203)
    D.   12 in (305)

Solution

In residential buildings, the minimum thickness for a concrete slab on grade is about 4 in (102). It could be as thick as 8 in (203) in industrial buildings and warehouses with heavy live loads.

The answer is B.

56. Which of the following statements about a concrete slab on grade is FALSE?

    A.   A slab on grade is generally placed on compacted soil or a layer of gravel.
    B.   A slab on grade does not require any reinforcement, therefore unreinforced concrete is always used.
    C.   A slab on grade is generally reinforced with welded wire fabric.
    D.   Post-tensioning can be used in slabs on grade.

Solution

The false statement is B. A slab on grade is directly supported by the ground and generally carries little structural stress. Theoretically, it only needs reinforcement for the control of cracking due to temperature stresses and shrinkage. However, due to uneven loading and the difficulty in getting a uniformly stiff base, reinforcement also helps control cracks due to bending and shear.

To place a slab on grade, topsoil is generally scraped to expose the subsoil beneath, then a 4 in (102) layer of crushed stone is compacted over the subsoil as a drainage layer. A moisture barrier is laid over the crushed stone. A layer of sand is generally recommended over the moisture barrier to absorb excess water from the concrete. A reinforced mesh of welded wire fabric is laid over the moisture barrier or sand. For lightly loaded slabs, such as in residential buildings, the welded wire fabric used has a wire spacing of 6 in (152) in each direction and a wire diameter of 0.135 inch (3.4). It is referred to as 6×6–W1.4×W1.4. For slabs in buildings with heavier loads, the welded wire fabric is made of heavier wires, or a grid of reinforcing bars could be used instead. Control joints at intervals must also be provided in a slab on grade.

Post-tensioning could also be used in a slab on grade, especially for slabs over unstable soils and for superflat floors. It provides a better resistance to cracking that can result from concentrated loads and other causes. It also eliminates the need for control joints, and could allow the use of a thinner slab.

The answer is B.

57.   A reinforced concrete one-way slab is 8 in (203) thick. For the main reinforcement used to resist bending moment, what is the maximum permissible spacing between reinforcing bars?

    A.   15 in (381)
    B.   18 in (457)
    C.   24 in (610)
    D.   40 in (1016)

Solution

ACI 318, Sec. 10.5.4, requires a maximum spacing between bars of the main reinforcement for bending of three times the slab thickness or 18 in (457), whichever is smaller. Based on this requirement, for an 8 in (457) slab the bar spacing of the main reinforcement should not exceed the smaller of 24 in (610) or 18 in (457). The maximum spacing is, therefore, 18 in (457).

The answer is B.

58.   Which of the following statements about the spacing of stirrups in reinforced concrete beams is true?

I.   The spacing of stirrups depends on the magnitude of the bending moments.
II.   The spacing of stirrups depends on the magnitude of shear forces.
III.   The spacing of stirrups should be 12 in (305).
IV.   The spacing of stirrups depends on the grades of steel and concrete used.

    A.   III only
    B.   I and II only
    C.   II and IV only
    D.   I, II, and IV only

Solution

The true statements are II and IV. The spacing of stirrups in reinforced concrete beams depends on the magnitude of shear forces. Stirrups are placed to help resist shear. They generally carry the amount of shear that cannot be resisted by the concrete alone. The stirrup spacing is also a function of the grades of concrete and steel used. For both materials, higher grades better resist shear stress than lower grades. For example, stirrups made with grade 60 steel can resist more shear stress than those made from grade 40 steel.

The answer is C.

WALLS AND RETAINING WALLS

59.   Cast-in-place reinforced concrete walls are used for

I.   bearing walls
II.   shear walls
III.   fire walls
IV.   nonbearing partitions

    A.   I and II only
    B.   I and IV only
    C.   I, II, and III only
    D.   II, III, and IV only

Solution

Cast-in-place reinforced concrete walls are used for bearing, shear, and fire walls. Cast-in-place concrete is unsuited for nonbearing partitions because of its weight, the cost of forms, and the difficulty of installation after the floors are built.

The answer is C.

60.   Which of the following statements about concrete walls are true? (Choose the four that apply.)

    A.   Concrete has replaced stone and brick for foundation walls because it is more economical and more watertight.
    B.   Concrete foundation walls are often reinforced at a large reinforcement ratio.
    C.   Plain (unreinforced) concrete foundation walls withstand uneven settlement without serious cracking better than brick masonry walls do.
    D.   Columns may rest on a concrete bearing wall.
    E.   Foundation walls must resist vertical loads and lateral earth pressure.
    F.   Reinforcement in concrete foundation walls is necessary for temperature, shrinkage and uneven settlement.

Solution

Option B is false. Concrete foundation walls are frequently reinforced to better withstand temperature change, shrinkage, and uneven settlement, though reinforcement may be minimal.

Option C is also false. Brick masonry foundation walls withstand uneven settlement without serious cracking better than plain concrete.

The answer is A, D, E, and F.

61.   What is the general distance of reinforcement bar spacing for reinforced brick masonry walls?

    A.   less than 10 in (less than 250)
    B.   from 10 in to 14 in (250 to 360)
    C.   from 18 in to 36 in (460 to 910)
    D.   from 36 in to 50 in (910 to 1270)

Solution

Reinforcement bar spacing in reinforced brick masonry walls is generally 18 in to 36 in (460 to 910). Reinforced brick masonry walls consist of two wythes of bricks with a grouted space in between that is about 2 in (50) wide. Vertical and horizontal no. 4 or no. 5 rebars are normally placed in this space.

The answer is C.

62.   In the design of a retaining wall, and according to most codes, the minimum safety factor to consider for sliding is

    A.   1.2
    B.   1.5
    C.   2.0
    D.   3.0

Solution

In the design of a retaining wall, and according to most codes, the minimum safety factor to consider for sliding is 1.5. A factor of 2.0 is generally considered for overturning.

The answer is B.

63.   Retaining walls may be made of

I.   sitecast or precast concrete
II.   masonry
III.   preservative-treated wood
IV.   galvanized steel

    A.   I only
    B.   I and II only
    C.   I, II, and III only
    D.   I, II, III, and IV

Solution

Retaining walls could be made of any of the listed materials. Sitecast concrete retaining walls are the most common.

The answer is D.

FOUNDATION SYSTEMS

64.   Which of the following statements about caissons is FALSE?

    A.   Caissons are concrete cylinders poured into drilled holes.
    B.   Caissons are steel or concrete cylinders that are hammered or driven into the earth.
    C.   Caissons extend through weak soils to bear on a hard stratum.
    D.   Caissons generally flare at the bottom to achieve the required bearing area.

Solution

Caissons consist of concrete that is poured (not hammered or driven) into drilled holes. (*Piles* are cylinders driven into the earth by hammering.) Statement B is false.

A caisson is, in a way, similar to a column footing. It transfers the load from a column over a soil area large enough so that the allowable bearing capacity of the soil is not exceeded. However, a caisson, unlike a column footing, extends through layers of weak soil until it reaches a satisfactory bearing layer, such as rock or dense sand and gravel. It is constructed by drilling a hole and flaring it out at the bottom as necessary, then filling it with concrete. Large auger drills are usually used for drilling holes for caissons. A temporary cylindrical steel casing is often lowered around the drill to support the soil around the hole. The hole is then filled with concrete and the casing is withdrawn. A *socketed caisson* is drilled into rock or firm soil, and transfers its load through friction between the soil and the sides of the caisson. It does not need to flare out at the bottom like a regular caisson.

The answer is B.

65. Friction piles are generally driven

  A. to a firm soil beneath
  B. to bedrock
  C. into soft materials, not necessarily to a firm layer
  D. to a depth of 100 ft (30.5 m)

Solution

An *end bearing pile* is generally driven by hammering the pile until it meets bedrock or other firm layer of soil. A *friction pile* develops its load-carrying capacity through friction between the sides of the pile and the soil through which it is driven, and does not need to be driven to a dense layer of soil.

The answer is C.

66. What shapes are used for steel piles?

I.   H shapes
II. round pipes
III. square tubes
IV. rectangular tubes

  A. I and II only
  B. I and III only
  C. I, II, and IV only
  D. I, II, III, and IV

Solution

The shapes used for steel piles are H shapes and round pipes. The H-piles are wide-flange sections, hot rolled, 8 in (203) to 14 in (356) deep. The cross section is approximately square. They are generally used in end-bearing piles. Steel pipe piles with diameters of 8 in (203) to 16 in (406) are also used. The lower end of the pipe may be open, or closed with a heavy steel plate. An open pile is easier to drive than a closed one, but its interior must be cleaned and inspected before it is filled with concrete.

The answer is A.

67. The most common cause of destructive differential settlement is

  A. bad construction
  B. inferior quality of materials
  C. nonuniform soil and/or foundation
  D. insufficient loadbearing capacity of the soil near the surface

Solution

The most common cause of differential settlement is nonuniform soil conditions, which can cause different areas and elements of a structure to settle at different rates. Other causes relate to the condition and loading of the foundation, such as a damaged foundation or broken piles. All buildings and structures are expected to settle slightly. Uniform settlement is seldom a problem. Problems caused by differential settlement include higher stress to structural elements that were not designed for the additional stress, and cracking in surface finishes.

The answer is C.

68. A column is supported on a group of four drilled piles, each with a 16 in diameter. The column carries a total load of 160 kips. The frictional capacity of each pile is 400 psf. What is the required depth for each pile?

  A. 4 ft
  B. 10 ft
  C. 21 ft
  D. 24 ft

Solution

The load supported by each pile is

$$P = \frac{\text{total column load}}{\text{number of piles}}$$

$$= \frac{160 \text{ kips}}{4}$$

$$= 40 \text{ kips}$$

The required frictional area (A_{req}) for one pile is calculated by dividing the load per pile by the given frictional resistance of each pile.

$$A_{req} = \frac{40 \text{ kips}}{0.400 \ \dfrac{\text{kips}}{\text{ft}^2}} = 100 \text{ ft}^2$$

The radius (r) of the 16 in diameter pile is half the diameter, or 8 in (0.67 ft). The circumference of the circular pile is given by

$$C = 2\pi r$$

$$= 2\pi(0.67 \text{ ft})$$

$$= 4.2 \text{ ft}$$

The surface area in contact with the soil (A_{req}) is equal to the circumference of the pile multiplied by the required pile depth (d).

$$A_{req} = 100 \text{ ft}^2$$

$$Cd = 100 \text{ ft}^2$$

$$(4.2 \text{ ft})d = 100 \text{ ft}^2$$

$$d = \frac{100 \text{ ft}^2}{4.2 \text{ ft}} = 23.81 \text{ ft} \quad (24 \text{ ft})$$

The answer is D.

CONNECTIONS

69.   The following illustration shows a welded connection in which a 3 in by $^3/_4$ in plate is connected to a 5 in by $^3/_4$ in plate by the maximum size of fillet weld permitted by the AISC Specifications. Both plates are made of ASTM A36 steel. The plate is subjected to a 38 kips tension force as shown. What are the size and length of the required weld using E70 electrodes? Use an allowable shear stress of 21 ksi for E70 electrodes.

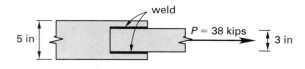

A.   weld size, $^1/_2$ in;
       weld length, 2 in on each side
B.   weld size, $^3/_4$ in;
       weld length, 2 in on each side
C.   weld size, $^{11}/_{16}$ in;
       weld length, 3 in on each side
D.   weld size, $^{11}/_{16}$ in;
       weld length, 4 in on each side

Solution

According to the AISC Specification, the largest size for a fillet weld is $^1/_{16}$ in less than the thickness of the material. Therefore, the largest fillet weld size for this connection is

$$\tfrac{3}{4} \text{ in} - \tfrac{1}{16} \text{ in} = \tfrac{11}{16} \text{ in}$$

The throat area per inch of weld length is

$$A = (\cos 45°)\left(\tfrac{11}{16} \text{ in}\right) = 0.486 \text{ in}^2$$

For E70 electrodes, the allowable shear stress is given as 21 ksi. The allowable load per inch of weld length is equal to the allowable shear stress multiplied by the throat area.

$$p = FA = \left(21 \frac{\text{kips}}{\text{in}^2}\right)(0.486 \text{ in}^2) = 10.21 \text{ kips/in of weld}$$

The total length of the weld is determined by dividing the total force acting on the connection by the allowable load per inch of weld length.

$$l = \frac{P}{p} = \frac{38 \text{ kips}}{10.21 \dfrac{\text{kips}}{\text{in}}} = 3.72 \text{ in}$$

The length of the weld on each side of the plate is the total required weld length divided by 2.

$$\frac{3.72 \text{ in}}{2} = 1.86 \text{ in} \quad (2 \text{ in})$$

The AISC Specification requires a weld length at least equal to the perpendicular distance between welds, which in this case is 3 in. Therefore, the weld length should be the minimum required length of 3 in on each side.

The answer is C.

70.   What is the shear bolt value for a 1 in diameter bolt of A307 steel, assuming standard holes and single shear in a bearing-type connection? Use Table 2, Shear Bolt Values, in the Appendix.

A.   0.79 kips
B.   7.9 kips
C.   15.7 kips
D.   16.5 kips

Solution

To determine the shear bolt value for a 1 in diameter A307 bolt, refer to Table 2. Select A307 steel, listed under "ASTM designation" next to "bolts". From the top row, select the nominal diameter of 1 in. Under "hole type", select STD, for a standard round hole. Under "loading", select the letter S for single shear, and then read the value of 7.9 kips.

The answer is B.

71. Which of the following statements about steel connections is FALSE?

    A. Bolts are easily installed, inexpensive, and can be visually checked.

    B. One of the advantages of using welded studs is a reduction in the number of holes to be punched.

    C. Rivets are still fabricated on a limited basis.

    D. The overall cost of riveted construction is usually lower than the cost of using bolted or welded connections.

Solution

The overall cost of riveted construction is usually higher than the cost of construction using bolted or welded because of increased labor and equipment requirements. Statement D is false.

Rivets, though once popular, are not often used today, but they are still fabricated on a limited basis. A rivet has a cylindrical shank with a head at one end and excess metal at the other end. The shank extends through the parts to be connected and the remaining metal is compressed to form the other head. The head end is backed up by a pneumatic jackhammer. A second pneumatic hammer with a head-shaped die is used to form the second head.

The answer is D.

LATERAL FORCES: PRINCIPLES AND STRUCTURAL SYSTEMS

72. What type of irregularity is illustrated in the building plan shown?

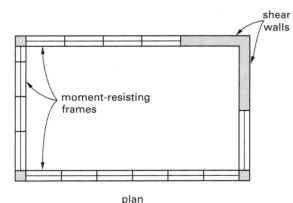

plan

    A. reentrant corner

    B. diaphragm discontinuity

    C. torsional irregularity

    D. column stiffness variation

Solution

The building plan illustrates torsional irregularity. *Torsion* is defined as the rotation or twisting in a diaphragm that results when the center of mass is different from the center of rigidity.

To minimize torsion, building designs are symmetrical and regular both in geometry and in stiffness. The building plan shown is geometrically symmetrical. However, it is not symmetrical in stiffness; one corner of the plan consists of shear walls, while the rest of the perimeter uses moment-resisting frames.

The answer is C.

73. What type of irregularity is illustrated in the building elevation shown?

elevation

    A. stiffness irregularity

    B. diaphragm discontinuity

    C. torsional irregularity

    D. column stiffness variation

Solution

The building elevation illustrates stiffness irregularity. The first story is a "soft story" because it is supported on columns, which creates a difference in stiffness from the rest of the building above. Bracing the columns would improve the condition.

A column stiffness variation results when the supporting columns on the first floor have different heights, as may be the case on a sloped site.

The answer is A.

74.   A revolving cup anemometer measures

    A.   wind pressure
    B.   wind speed
    C.   earthquake magnitude
    D.   wind forces

Solution

A *revolving cup anemometer* is used to measure wind speed by measuring the time it takes a 1 mi column of air to pass by it. This 1 mi distance is determined by the cup's revolutions.

The answer is B.

75.   In lateral load resisting systems, a steel frame is often used in conjunction with concrete shear walls. What type of load does each component of this system carry?

    A.   The steel frame carries most of the vertical gravity load, and the concrete shear walls carry the lateral load.
    B.   The steel frame carries the lateral load, and the concrete shear walls carry most of the vertical gravity load.
    C.   Both components carry the vertical and lateral loads equally.
    D.   The steel frame carries most of the vertical and lateral loads.

Solution

The steel frame carries most of the vertical gravity load, and the concrete shear walls carry the lateral load. This system is commonly used, and the concrete shear walls are often placed around the building's mechanical core, enclosing elevators and stairways. The shear walls transmit the lateral forces to the foundation and must be continuous.

The answer is A.

76.   Torsion

  I.   is rotation caused in a diaphragm when the center of mass does not coincide with the center of rigidity
  II.   is rotation caused in a diaphragm when the center of mass coincides with the center of rigidity
  III.   occurs only in flexible diaphragms
  IV.   occurs only in rigid diaphragms

    A.   I and III only
    B.   I and IV only
    C.   II and III only
    D.   II and IV only

Solution

Torsion is a rotation caused in a rigid diaphragm when the center of mass, where the resultant load is applied, does not coincide with the center of rigidity, where the resultant load is resisted. Torsional moments cause forces in the shear-resisting elements.

The answer is B.

77.   Braced frames resist lateral forces by developing

    A.   bending
    B.   shear
    C.   axial tension and compression
    D.   torsion

Solution

Braced frames resist lateral forces by developing axial tension and compression in the braces. The most common types of bracing are diagonal bracing and chevron bracing.

The answer is C.

78.   In order to provide for accidental torsion in a building that is 70 ft (20 m) wide and 120 ft (35 m) long, the International Building Code requires that the center of mass be offset

    A. by 3.5 ft (1 m) for the forces acting perpendicularly to the 70 ft (20 m) dimension and by 6 ft (1.8 m) for the forces acting in the other direction

    B. by 6 ft (1.8 m) for the forces acting perpendicularly to the 70 ft (20 m) dimension and by 3.5 ft (1 m) for the forces acting in the other direction

    C. by 7 ft (2 m) for the forces acting perpendicularly to the 70 ft (20 m) dimension and by 12 ft (3.5 m) for the forces acting in the other direction

    D. by 12 ft (3.5 m) for the forces acting perpendicularly to the 70 ft (20 m) dimension and by 6 ft (2 m) for the forces acting in the other direction

Solution

The International Building Code requires that seismic design be in accordance with ASCE 7. Section 12.8.4.2 of ASCE 7 requires that, when providing for accidental torsion, the mass at each level of a building is assumed to be displaced in each direction a distance equal to 5% of the building dimension at that level in the direction perpendicular to the direction of the force. This means that for a building that is 70 ft (20 m) wide and 120 ft (35 m) long, the calculated center of mass should be displaced by 3.5 ft (1.0 m) for the forces acting perpendicular to the 70 ft (20 m) dimension and by 6 ft (1.8 m) for the forces acting in the other direction.

These directions are reversed in choice B. Choices A and C are both calculated based on a 10% displacement instead of the 5% required by the code.

The answer is A.

79.   Which of the following lateral load resisting systems is the most flexible?

    A. a shear wall

    B. a braced frame with a concentric diagonal bracing

    C. a braced frame with a concentric chevron bracing

    D. a braced frame with an eccentric chevron bracing

Solution

There are generally two types of braced frames: concentric and eccentric. Concentric frames were used first, then the eccentric frames were developed with the objective of making braced frames more ductile and more flexible. The chevron bracing is a reversed V-shaped bracing. With eccentric chevron bracing, a small gap (called an eccentricity) is provided between the two braces at their top connection point, thereby creating more flexibility in the system.

The most flexible system among the listed options is a braced frame with an eccentric chevron bracing.

A shear wall is the most rigid lateral load resisting system. It resists lateral forces by developing shear in its own plane. A braced frame is a vertical truss that resists lateral loads by developing axial tension and compression in the truss members. A braced frame is more flexible than a shear wall.

The answer is D.

80.   Which of the following statements about special moment-resisting frames (SMRFs) are true?

    I.   SMRFs are designed and detailed to assure ductile behavior.

    II. SMRFs are built using structural steel only.

    III. SMRFs require special attention to details.

    IV. Any rigid frame built using structural steel is considered a SMRF.

    A. I and II only

    B. II and III only

    C. I, III, and IV only

    D. I, II, III, and IV

Solution

The true statements are I and III. Statements II and IV are false. A special moment-resisting frame (SMRF) is a rigid frame that is designed and detailed to ensure ductility and to be able to absorb a large amount of energy in the inelastic phase without failure or unacceptable deformation. Structural steel is not the only material used to construct SMRFs. These frames could also be built using reinforced concrete. Not all rigid frames built using structural steel qualify as SMRFs, which need to comply with special code requirements.

The answer is B.

81.   Which of the following statements about ordinary moment-resisting frames (OMRFs) is FALSE?

  A.   OMRFs don't have to meet special detailing requirements for ductile behavior.
  B.   OMRFs may only be built using structural steel.
  C.   OMRFs may be built using concrete or steel.
  D.   OMRFs have less stringent requirements than the special moment-resisting frames.

Solution

Ordinary moment-resisting frames (OMRFs) may be built using structural steel or reinforced concrete. Concrete OMRFs are permitted only in buildings assigned to seismic design categories A and B. Steel OMRFs are allowed without any limitations in buildings of seismic design categories A, B, and C. In seismic design categories D and higher, steel OMRFs are permitted under certain conditions only.

The answer is B.

82.   Which of the following statements about shear walls is FALSE?

  A.   A shear wall resists lateral load by developing shear in its own plane.
  B.   A shear wall could develop some bending or flexural stresses in addition to shear stress.
  C.   Shear walls may not be built using masonry, whether reinforced or not.
  D.   Shear walls may be constructed using steel or wood stud walls.

Solution

Shear walls may be built using reinforced masonry. The materials used to construct shear walls are reinforced concrete, steel, reinforced masonry, and wood stud walls with a facing of plywood, particleboard, or fiberboard. A shear wall resists lateral loads by developing shear in its own plane. In addition to the shear stress, it can also develop bending stress.

The answer is C.

83.   Diaphragms made of steel deck generally have allowable shear values of

  A.   less than 100 lbf/ft (1.46 kN/m)
  B.   100 lbf/ft to 2600 lbf/ft (1.46 kN/m to 37.9 kN/m)
  C.   3000 lbf/ft to 5000 lbf/ft (43.8 kN/m to 73.0 kN/m)
  D.   10,000 lbf/ft to 12,000 lbf/ft (146 kN/m to 175 kN/m)

Solution

Diaphragms made of steel deck have allowable shear values that vary between 100 lbf/ft and 2600 lbf/ft (1.46 kN/m and 37.9 kN/m).

The answer is B.

84.   Which of the following factors affect the allowable shear value in a diaphragm system made of steel deck?

  I.   thickness of the steel deck
  II.   size of welds and other connections between deck and framing
  III. spacing of welds and other connections between deck and framing
  IV.   presence of concrete topping

  A.   I only
  B.   I and IV only
  C.   I, II, and III only
  D.   I, II, III, and IV

Solution

All the factors listed in the four statements have an effect on the allowable shear value of a diaphragm made of steel deck.

The answer is D.

85.   In order to limit the horizontal deflection of a plywood diaphragm system, building codes generally limit the span-to-depth ratio of the diaphragm to

  A.   2:1
  B.   3:1
  C.   4:1
  D.   5:1

Solution

Building codes limit the span-to-depth ratio of a plywood diaphragm to 4:1. This prevents excessive horizontal deflection of the diaphragm. Codes also require that diaphragm deflection be controlled in a way that will not exceed the limits for structural integrity of the diaphragm and the attached load-resisting elements. Excessive horizontal deflection of the diaphragm might lead to damage or failure of the attached resisting elements.

The answer is C.

86.   What are the support reactions of the truss loaded with a lateral load of 12 kips (12 kN) and a gravity load of 20 kips (20 kN) as shown in the figure below?

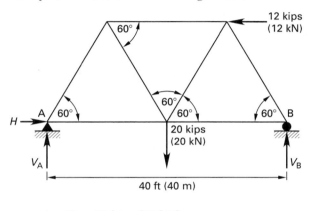

A. $H = 12$ kips (12 kN),
    $V_A = 4.8$ kips (4.8 kN)
    $V_B = 15.2$ kips (15.2 kN)
B. $H = 12$ kips (12 kN)
    $V_A = 15.2$ kips (15.2 kN)
    $V_B = 4.8$ kips (4.8 kN)
C. $H = 12$ kips (12 kN)
    $V_A = 10$ kips (10 kN)
    $V_B = 10$ kips (10 kN)
D. $H = 20$ kips (20 kN)
    $V_A = 16$ kips (16 kN)
    $V_B = 16$ kips (16 kN)

Solution

The support reactions are found by solving the three equations of equilibrium for the truss.

$$\Sigma F_x = 0$$
$$\Sigma F_y = 0$$
$$\Sigma M = 0$$

The sum of moments may be taken about either support A or B. Clockwise moments are considered positive, and counterclockwise moments are considered negative.

The span of the truss is given as 40, and all angles are 60°. Therefore, the height of the truss (h) can be calculated using the span and the angles.

$$h = (10)(\tan 60°) = 17.32$$

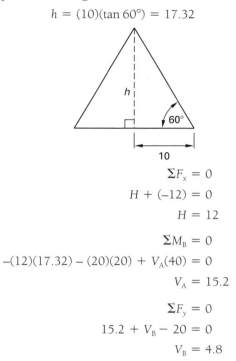

$$\Sigma F_x = 0$$
$$H + (-12) = 0$$
$$H = 12$$

$$\Sigma M_B = 0$$
$$-(12)(17.32) - (20)(20) + V_A(40) = 0$$
$$V_A = 15.2$$

$$\Sigma F_y = 0$$
$$15.2 + V_B - 20 = 0$$
$$V_B = 4.8$$

The answer is B.

87.   Which of the following types of diaphragms has the largest allowable shear value?

A. a blocked plywood diaphragm with a ³/₈ in (9.5) panel of structural I-grade
B. an unblocked plywood diaphragm with a ³/₈ in (9.5) panel of structural I-grade
C. a diaphragm made of steel deck with a 2 in (51) concrete topping
D. a diaphragm that consists of a 6 in (152) concrete slab

Solution

Of the listed diaphragm types, the diaphragm that consists of a 6 in (152) concrete slab has the largest allowable shear value. Such a slab would have an allowable shear of about 10,000 lbf/ft (146 kN/m). A diaphragm made of steel deck has an allowable shear between 100 lbf/ft and 2600 lbf/ft (1.46 kN/m and 37.9 kN/m). Plywood diaphragms generally have an allowable shear value between 100 lbf/ft and 800 lbf/ft (1.46 kN/m and 11.7 kN/m).

The answer is D.

88. Which of the following connections offers the best resistance to lateral loads?

    A. a pinned steel beam-to-column connection using steel framing angles

    B. a pinned steel beam-to-column connection using flexible beam seats

    C. a connection between a cast-in-place concrete beam and cast-in-place concrete column

    D. a typical connection between a precast concrete column and a precast concrete beam

Solution

The sitecast (or cast-in-place) concrete beam-to-column connection is the one that offers the best resistance for lateral loads. Cast-in-place concrete construction is a monolithic construction that creates rigid moment-resisting connections between elements. These connections generally resist lateral forces better compared to flexible steel connections and typical precast connections.

The answer is C.

SEISMIC DESIGN

89. On the Richter scale, compared to a magnitude 6 earthquake, an earthquake of magnitude 8 releases about

    A. 32 times as much energy
    B. 100 times as much energy
    C. 1000 times as much energy
    D. 10,000 times as much energy

Solution

An earthquake of magnitude 8 on the Richter scale releases about 1000 times as much energy as an earthquake of magnitude 6. The Richter scale is a logarithmic scale. An earthquake of magnitude 7 on this scale has ten times the horizontal shaking amplitude, and releases about 32 times as much energy, as an earthquake of magnitude 6. And an earthquake of magnitude 8 releases 1000 (about 32 × 32) times the energy released by a magnitude 6 quake.

The answer is C.

90. The most damaging effect of earthquakes is

    A. ground shaking
    B. landslides
    C. soil liquefaction
    D. avalanches

Solution

The most damaging effect of earthquakes is ground shaking or vibration because this covers a large area. Vibrations can occur in any direction, including vertically. Current practice, however, is to neglect the vertical component and consider only horizontal or lateral movement. The vertical component of vibration is generally small compared to the horizontal one, and the weight of the building also serves to counteract it.

The answer is A.

91. Which of the following regions of the United States are most vulnerable to earthquakes?

    A. Florida and the Gulf Coast
    B. Alaska and areas west of the Rockies
    C. New York and the Northeast
    D. Indiana and Illinois

Solution

California, Alaska, and locations west of the Rockies are the regions of the United States most vulnerable to earthquakes. The Alaska earthquake of 1964 measured 8.4 on the Richter scale. The San Fernando earthquake of 1971 was 6.4. The San Francisco earthquake of 1989 measured 7.1, and the 1994 Northridge earthquake that hit the Los Angeles area registered 6.7.

The answer is B.

92. The largest earthquakes ever recorded worldwide have a magnitude on the Richter scale of approximately

    A. 6.5
    B. 7.5
    C. 8.5
    D. 9.5

Solution

The largest magnitude earthquakes ever recorded on the Richter scale worldwide are approximately 9.5. One such earthquake hit Chile in 1960, causing 5000 deaths. The magnitude of the 1964 Alaska earthquake was 9.2.

(By comparison, the magnitude of the 1906 San Francisco earthquake was 8.3.)

Earthquakes occur mostly at the boundaries of tectonic plates, in zones where one plate slides past another. Many are concentrated along the Ring of Fire, a 24,000 mi (38 600 km) long band that coincides with the margins of the Pacific Ocean. The Japan earthquake of 1933 measured 8.9 on the Richter scale, and the one that hit Kobe, Japan, in 1995 measured 6.9.

Another setting for tectonic earthquakes is a zone stretching across the Mediterranean and Caspian seas and the Himalayas, ending in the Bay of Bengal. Quakes in this area have devastated parts of Portugal, Algeria, Morocco, Italy, Greece, the Balkans, Turkey, Iran, and India.

The answer is D.

93.   Which of the following statements are true?

I.   For a very rigid structure, the maximum acceleration of the structure is almost equal to the ground acceleration.

II.   A flexible building has a longer period of vibration and a lower maximum acceleration than a rigid structure.

III.   A building's acceleration is generally greater on dense soil than it is on soft soil.

IV.   Increasing the stiffness of a building increases its natural period of vibration.

    A.   I only
    B.   I and II only
    C.   II and III only
    D.   III and IV only

Solution

The true statements are I and II. Statement III is false. A building's acceleration is generally greater on soft soil than on dense soil. Statement IV is also false. Increasing the stiffness of the building decreases its natural period of vibration.

The answer is B.

94.   As a structure's period of vibration increases, its peak acceleration also increases. It reaches its maximum value when the period of vibration is approximately

    A.   0.5 sec
    B.   1.0 sec
    C.   2.0 sec
    D.   5.0 sec

Solution

The peak acceleration of a building or a structure increases as the structure's period increases, and it reaches a maximum when the period is 0.5 sec. This is one of the conclusions drawn from the response spectra.

A response spectrum is basically a graph that shows, for different soil types, the relation between the ratio of building acceleration to ground acceleration and the period (T) in seconds.

The answer is A.

95.   A water treatment plant has a short-period response acceleration of 0.20 and its 1 sec period response acceleration is 0.10. Use Tables 3 and 4 in the Appendix, Seismic Design Category Based on Short-Period and 1-Second Response Acceleration. Based on the IBC, what is the plant's seismic design category?

    A.   category A
    B.   category B
    C.   category C
    D.   category D

Solution

The seismic design category for this plant is C. According to the IBC, water treatment plants are in occupancy category III. Using Tables 3 and 4 and based on the given values of the short-period response acceleration (S_{DS}) and the 1 sec period response acceleration (S_{D1}) (0.20 and 0.1, respectively), and for an occupancy category III, the seismic design category is C.

The answer is C.

96. Which of the following structures are exempt from IBC seismic requirements?

I. detached one- and two-family homes located in areas where S_s is less than 0.4g

II. hospitals and health care facilities

III. minor agricultural storage structures

IV. wastewater treatment plants

    A. I only

    B. III only

    C. I and III only

    D. II, III, and IV only

Solution

The true statements are I and III. Of the options listed, the structures that are exempt from seismic requirements and that need not be designed according to the IBC are detached one- and two-family homes in areas where the mapped spectral response (S_s) is less than 0.4g, and minor agricultural storage facilities only incidentally occupied by humans.

The answer is C.

97. Seismic design category D corresponds to buildings and structures in areas

    A. close to major active faults

    B. where moderate ground shaking may occur

    C. where expected ground shaking is minor

    D. expected to experience severe and destructive ground shaking but not located close to major active fault lines

Solution

Seismic design category D corresponds to buildings and structures in areas expected to experience severe and destructive ground shaking but not located close to major active fault lines.

Seismic design category A corresponds to buildings in areas where expected ground shaking is minor.

Seismic design category B corresponds to buildings of occupancy categories I, II, and III, in areas where moderately destructive ground shaking is expected.

Seismic design category C corresponds to buildings of the occupancy category IV, in areas where moderately destructive ground shaking might take place, and to buildings of occupancy categories I, II, and III, in areas where a somewhat more severe ground shaking is expected.

Seismic design category E corresponds to buildings of occupancy categories I, II, and III in areas located near major active faults.

Seismic design category F corresponds to buildings of the occupancy category IV, in areas located near major active faults.

Table 5 in the Appendix shows the different occupancy categories of buildings and other structures according to the International Building Code (IBC).

The answer is D.

98. A three-story office building is built using steel moment-resisting frames. The total height of the building is 38 ft (11.6 m). The design spectral response acceleration parameter at 1 sec is given as 0.3. Using Tables 5 and 6 in the Appendix, what is the period of vibration for this building?

    A. 0.51 sec

    B. 0.72 sec

    C. 0.85 sec

    D. 1.0 sec

Solution

Calculate the period of vibration (T) according to the IBC equation

$$T = C_u T_a$$

C_u is the coefficient for the upper limit on the calculated period and it is given in Table 5 in the Appendix. It is a function of the design spectral response acceleration parameter (S_{D1}) given in the problem as 0.3. From Table 6, C_u is 1.4 for both U.S. and SI units.

T_a is the approximate period of vibration given by the equation

$$T_a = C_t h_n^x$$

C_t and x are called the approximate period parameters. They are coefficients that depend on the structural system, and are given in Table 6 in the Appendix. For steel moment-resisting frames, x is 0.8 for both U.S. and SI units, and C_t is 0.028 (0.0724 in SI units).

In U.S. units:

$$T_a = C_t h_n^x$$
$$= (0.028)(38 \text{ ft})^{0.8}$$
$$= 0.514 \text{ sec}$$
$$T = C_u T_a$$
$$= (1.4)(0.514 \text{ sec})$$
$$= 0.72 \text{ sec}$$

In SI units:

$$T_a = C_t h_n^x$$
$$= (0.0724)(11.6 \text{ m})^{0.8}$$
$$= 0.514 \text{ s}$$
$$T = C_u T_a$$
$$= (1.4)(0.514 \text{ s})$$
$$= 0.72 \text{ s}$$

The answer is B.

99.   A building is to be constructed on a site that is mainly comprised of soft rock and dense soil (site class C). The mapped spectral response acceleration at the short period of 0.2 sec (S_S) is given as 0.50, and the mapped spectral response acceleration at the 1 sec period (S_1) is given as 0.2. Using Tables 8 and 9 in the Appendix, what are the design spectral response values S_{DS} and S_{D1}?

A. $S_{DS} = 0.40$ and $S_{D1} = 0.21$
B. $S_{DS} = 0.80$ and $S_{D1} = 1.1$
C. $S_{DS} = 1.2$ and $S_{D1} = 1.6$
D. $S_{DS} = 1.5$ and $S_{D1} = 1.8$

Solution

The values of the design spectral response are

$$S_{DS} = \tfrac{2}{3} F_a S_S$$
$$S_{D1} = \tfrac{2}{3} F_v S_1$$

The mapped spectral response accelerations are given in the problem. S_S is given as 0.5 and S_1 is given as 0.2. The value of F_a is taken from Table 8 using site class C and is 1.2. The value of F_v is taken from Table 9 using site class C and is 1.6. The above equations and values are the same for both U.S. and SI units.

$$S_{DS} = \tfrac{2}{3} (1.2)(0.5) = 0.40$$
$$S_{D1} = \tfrac{2}{3} (1.6)(0.2) = 0.21$$

The answer is A.

100.   A two-story small residential building is being planned. The structure is to be 26 ft (7.9 m) high. A bearing wall system with regular concrete shear walls is being used. The estimated seismic weight of the building is 3000 kips (12 000 kN). The seismic response coefficient is calculated as 0.04. The base shear for this building rounded to the nearest whole number is _____ kips (_____ kN). (Fill in the blank.)

Solution

The base shear (V) is given by the IBC equation

$$V = C_s W$$

The seismic response coefficient (C_s) is given in the problem as 0.04. The seismic weight of the building (W) is given as 3000 kips (12 000 kN).

In U.S. units:

$$V = C_s W = (0.04)(3000 \text{ kips}) = 120 \text{ kips}$$

In SI units:

$$V = C_s W = (0.04)(12\,000 \text{ kN}) = 480 \text{ kN}$$

The answer is 120 kips (480 kN).

101.   Which of the following buildings are equipped with base isolators?

I.   Sears Tower in Chicago
II.   Walt Disney Concert Hall in Los Angeles
III. the International Terminal at San Francisco's International Airport
IV.   Los Angeles City Hall

A.   I only
B.   II and III only
C.   III and IV only
D.   II, III, and IV only

Solution

The International Terminal at San Francisco's International Airport, which opened in 2000, and the Los Angeles City Hall are equipped with base isolators.

Base isolators are designed to isolate the structure from the ground in order to reduce the effect of ground motion on the structure. They consist of dampers and steel bearings placed at the base of columns. Base isolators reduce the building's acceleration due to ground shaking and absorb the earthquake energy. Based on experience, base isolation seems to be effective. In Japan, buildings equipped with base isolators often survive earthquakes without any damage.

The Los Angeles City Hall was built in 1928 and is a land-mark building. It was retrofitted in 1995, at which time the building was lifted up and placed on base isolators. The International Terminal at San Francisco's International Airport was built on base isolators placed at the bottom of its columns. It is the largest building on base isolators in the world.

The Walt Disney Concert Hall in Los Angeles was designed by architect Frank Gehry. Although located in a high-risk seismic zone, the concert hall is not built on base isolators. This building was under construction when the Northridge earthquake hit the Los Angeles area in 1994. The garage was being built at the time, but was not damaged by the earthquake. The concert hall was originally designed with steel moment-resisting frames to resist lateral loads. During the Northridge earthquake many girder-to-column connections in steel moment-resisting frames failed, and the use of these frames was questioned. As a result, a portion of the California Building Code was suspended. Due to this, the structural engineers of the concert hall, the Los Angeles firm of John A. Martin & Associates, explored different solutions to the structural system, including adding base isolation to the frames. Ultimately, the engineers decided to use structural steel braced frames as a lateral load resisting system.

The answer is C.

WIND DESIGN

102. Wind speed is

    A.   slower near the ground surface
    B.   faster near the ground surface
    C.   the same at the ground surface as at 33 ft
         (10 m) above the ground surface
    D.   not related to the distance from the ground surface

Solution

Wind speed varies with the height above the ground surface. It is slower near the surface of the ground due to friction.

The answer is A.

103. What type of wind pressure is the roof of a building generally subject to?

    A.   direct (positive) pressure
    B.   uplift, or suction
    C.   drag forces
    D.   a combination of direct (positive) pressure and suction

Solution

The roof of a building is generally subject to uplift, or suction. This is why roofs are often blown off during hurricanes and tornadoes.

The answer is B.

104. A tropical storm with a wind speed of 80 mph (129 km/h) would be classified on the Saffir-Simpson scale as a

    A.   category 1 hurricane
    B.   category 2 hurricane
    C.   category 3 hurricane
    D.   category 4 hurricane

Solution

A tropical storm with a wind speed of 80 mph (129 km/h) is generally classified as a category 1 hurricane on the Saffir-Simpson scale. The table below summarizes the five categories of this scale.

	wind speeds mph (km/h)	storm surge, above normal ft (m)
category 1	74 to 95 (119 to 153)	4 to 5 (about 1.2 to 1.5)
category 2	96 to 110 (154 to 178)	6 to 8 (about 1.8 to 2.4)
category 3	111 to 130 (179 to 209)	9 to 12 (about 2.7 to 3.7)
category 4	131 to 155 (211 to 249)	13 to 18 (about 4.0 to 5.5)
category 5	greater than 155 (greater than 249)	greater than 18 (greater than 5.5)

The answer is A.

105. What is the lowest value of basic wind speed on the U.S. wind map provided by the International Building Code?

    A. 70 mph (31 m/s)
    B. 80 mph (36 m/s)
    C. 85 mph (38 m/s)
    D. 90 mph (40 m/s)

Solution

The lowest value of basic wind speed on the U.S. wind map given by the International Building Code is 85 mph (38 m/s). This value is assigned to an area that includes most of the West Coast of the United States, with the exception of the special wind regions there.

The answer is C.

106. The rotational wind speed in a tornado may exceed

    A. 100 mph (160 km/h)
    B. 200 mph (320 km/h)
    C. 300 mph (480 km/h)
    D. 500 mph (800 km/h)

Solution

The rotational speed in a tornado may exceed 500 mph (800 km/h), and averages about 250 mph (about 400 km/h).

The answer is D.

107. Which of the following structures require some complex wind calculations and possibly some wind tunnel testing? (Choose the three that apply.)

    A. a commercial building with a total height of 50 ft (15 m)
    B. a residential building with a height of 200 ft (61 m)
    C. an office building with a height of 450 ft (137 m)
    D. a building with a height-to-width ratio of 3
    E. a building with a height-to-width ratio of 7
    F. an extra-long span suspension bridge

Solution

An office building with a height of 450 ft (137 m), a building with a height-to-width ratio of 7, and an extra-long span suspension bridge would require some complex wind calculations and possibly some wind tunnel testing.

Generally, complex wind calculations and wind tunnel testing are required for buildings with heights exceeding 400 ft (122 m), for buildings subject to dynamic effects, those sensitive to wind vibrations, and for buildings with a height-to-width ratio of 5 or more. Wind tunnel testing is also often carried out on reduced-scale models of long-span suspension bridges.

The answer is C, E, and F.

108. Which of the following methods could be used to calculate wind pressures on the various building surfaces of a gabled rigid-frame building?

    A. only the normal force method
    B. only the projected area method
    C. either one of the two methods could be used
    D. neither the normal force method nor the projected area method could be used

Solution

Only the normal force method could be used for gabled rigid-frame buildings. In this method, the wind pressures are considered normal or perpendicular to the external surfaces. The normal force method can be used for any structure.

In the projected area method, wind pressures are considered acting on the projected horizontal and vertical areas of the building. This method is simplified and somewhat limited. It is generally used for structures less than 60 ft (18.3 m) high, and for buildings that are symmetrical and of a simple diaphragm. Also, when applying the projected area method, buildings must not be subject to any special wind considerations.

The answer is A.

109. Which two statements about designing for wind forces are correct?

I.   Maximum drift should be limited to 1/500 of a building's height.

II. Maximum drift should be limited to 1/100 of a building's height.

III. Drift between adjacent stories should be limited to 0.025 times the story height.

IV. Drift between adjacent stories should be limited to 0.0025 times the story height.

    A.   I and III

    B.   I and IV

    C.   II and III

    D.   II and IV

Solution

Maximum drift should be limited to 1/500 of a building's height, and drift between stories should be limited to 0.0025 times the story height.

The answer is B.

110. What is the gradient height?

    A.   the height above which ground friction and other obstructions stop affecting wind speed

    B.   the standard height at which wind measurements are supposed to be performed at different wind stations

    C.   a height above which wind speed becomes equal to wind speed near the ground

    D.   a height above which wind speed starts to decrease

Solution

The *gradient height* is the height above which ground friction and other obstructions no longer reduce wind speed. This is not the same as the standard height for wind measurements, 33 ft (10 m). The gradient height depends on the type of area (open, suburban, or urban). For example, the minimum gradient height for open country areas is 900 ft (270 m).

The answer is A.

111. In designing buildings and structures for wind forces, the ASCE/SEI 7 standard defines three different wind exposure categories: B, C, and D. In which category is the wind most severe?

    A.   category B

    B.   category C

    C.   category D

    D.   All three exposure categories have the same severity.

Solution

The most severe wind exposure is in category D, which refers to flat and unobstructed terrain near large bodies of water. Category B refers to urban and suburban wooded areas and terrain with obstructions. Category C refers to open terrain, such as in a desert area.

The answer is C.

112.   A small, one-story commercial building with a total height of 14 ft (4.3 m) is to be built on a flat site on the shore in the area of San Francisco. The building is to have a flat roof and a rectangular floor plan of 40 ft by 20 ft (12 m by 6 m). Use Figure 1, Basic Wind Speed, and Table 10, Wall Pressure Coefficients, in the Appendix. The formula for design wind pressure is

$$P = qGC_p - q_i(GC_{pi})$$

Use a basic wind velocity pressure, q, of 16.2 psf (775 N/m²). The gust factor, G, for rigid structures is 0.85. Using Method 2 from ASCE/SEI 7, what is the approximate design wind pressure acting outward on the leeward wall? Assume that the wind direction is parallel to the long side of the building.

    A.   4.1 psf (200 N/m²)

    B.   6.1 psf (290 N/m²)

    C.   8.1 psf (390 N/m²)

    D.   9.6 psf (460 N/m²)

Solution

According to ASCE/SEI 7, the design wind pressure on a building surface is given by

$$P = qGC_p - q_i(GC_{pi})$$

In U.S. units:

The basic wind velocity pressure, q, is given as 16.2 psf.

The internal pressure contributions are ignored (that is, GC_{pi} equals zero) because the section of the building is symmetrical. The design wind pressure equation becomes

$$P = qGC_p$$

The G factor (gust factor) takes into consideration both atmospheric and aerodynamic effects. The value of G is given as 0.85 for rigid structures.

C_p takes into account the differing effects of wind on various parts of the building. It is called the *external pressure coefficient*. The value of C_p is from Table 10, using Method 2 from ASCE/SEI 7. For a leeward wall, this value is 0.3 for an L/B (length-to-width ratio) of 2.

Substituting into the equation gives

$$P = \left(16.2 \, \frac{\text{lbf}}{\text{ft}^2}\right)(0.85)(-0.3) = -4.13 \text{ lbf/ft}^2 \quad (-4.1 \text{ psf})$$

This is a pressure of 4.1 psf acting outward on the leeward wall.

In SI units:

The basic wind velocity pressure, q, is already given as 775 N/m².

The internal pressure contributions are ignored (i.e., GC_i equals zero) because the section of the building is symmetrical. The design wind pressure equation becomes

$$P = qGC_p$$

The G factor (gust factor) takes into consideration both atmospheric and aerodynamic effects. The value of G is given as 0.85 for rigid structures.

C_p takes into account the differing effects of wind on various parts of the building. It is called the *external pressure coefficient*. The value of C_p is from Table 10, using Method 2 from ASCE/SEI 7. For a leeward wall, this value is 0.3 for an L/B (length-to-width ratio) of 2.

Substituting in the equation gives

$$P = \left(775 \, \frac{\text{N}}{\text{m}^2}\right)(0.85)(-0.3) = -197.63 \text{ N/m}^2 \quad (-200 \text{ N/m}^2)$$

This is a pressure of 200 N/m² acting outward on the leeward wall.

The answer is A.

113. For a building designed for downtown Newark, New Jersey, what is the wind exposure category according to the International Building Code?

    A. exposure B

    B. exposure C

    C. exposure D

    D. exposure E

Solution

A building in downtown Newark, New Jersey, would be in the wind exposure category B. According to the International Building Code (IBC), a site in the downtown area of a city would be classified as exposure B, which is the least severe exposure.

There are three exposure categories in the IBC.

- **Exposure B** is the least severe exposure, and generally relates to urban and suburban areas, wooded areas, and other terrain with numerous closely spaced obstructions the size of single-family dwellings or larger.

- **Exposure C** is generally for open terrain with scattered obstructions having heights of less than 30 ft (about 9 m), including flat open country, grasslands, and all water surfaces in hurricane-prone regions.

- **Exposure D** is the most severe exposure, and generally applies to flat, unobstructed areas, shorelines, and water surfaces outside hurricane-prone regions. It includes smooth mud flats, salt flats, and unbroken ice. Exposure D extends inland from the shoreline for a distance of 600 ft (183 m) or 20 times the height of the proposed building, whichever is greater.

The answer is A.

114. A small residential building is located on a flat site in an area with a basic wind speed is 85 mph (38 m/s). The basic wind velocity pressure on the windward wall is 9.0 psf (430 N/m²). If the building were located in an area with a 90 mph (40 m/s) basic wind speed and the same exposure category, what would be the approximate basic wind pressure on the same windward wall?

    A. 6.9 psf (330 N/m²)

    B. 8.0 psf (380 N/m²)

    C. 10 psf (480 N/m²)

    D. 11 psf (530 N/m²)

Solution

The basic wind velocity pressure, q, for the building at the second location is 10 psf (480 N/m²).

The basic wind velocity pressure is given by

$$q = 0.00256K_zK_{zt}K_dv^2I \quad \text{[U.S. units]}$$

$$q = 0.613K_zK_{zt}K_dv^2I \quad \text{[SI units]}$$

For two sites having the same exposure category, the factor K_z is the same. For a flat site, the factor K_{zt} is equal to 1. The directionality factor, K_d, is equal to 0.85 for buildings, so K_d is the same for both locations. The importance factor, I, is 1 for both cases, because the small residential building is considered occupancy category II.

Thus, the only factor in the equation that is different for the two locations is the wind velocity, v. In U.S. units or SI units,

$$\frac{q_1}{q_2} = \frac{v_1^2}{v_2^2}$$

q_1 and q_2 represent the basic wind velocity pressure at the first and second locations, respectively. v_1 and v_2 are the wind velocities at the first and second locations, respectively.

In U.S. units:

Solving for the wind pressure at the second location,

$$q_2 = \frac{q_1v_2^2}{v_1^2}$$

$$= \frac{\left(9.0 \dfrac{\text{lbf}}{\text{ft}^2}\right)\left(90 \dfrac{\text{mi}}{\text{hr}}\right)^2}{\left(85 \dfrac{\text{mi}}{\text{hr}}\right)^2}$$

$$= 10.09 \text{ lbf/ft}^2 \quad (10 \text{ psf})$$

In SI units:

Solving for the wind pressure at the second location,

$$q_2 = \frac{q_1v_2^2}{v_1^2}$$

$$= \frac{\left(430 \dfrac{\text{N}}{\text{m}^2}\right)\left(40 \dfrac{\text{m}}{\text{s}}\right)^2}{\left(38 \dfrac{\text{m}}{\text{s}}\right)^2}$$

$$= 476.45 \text{ N/m}^2 \quad (480 \text{ N/m}^2)$$

The answer is C.

---

115. A building located in which of the following areas would be in the most severe wind exposure category?

    A. downtown New York City

    B. on the shore near San Francisco

    C. a desert near Los Angeles

    D. downtown Seattle

Solution

A building located on the shore near San Francisco would be in exposure category D, which is the most severe exposure. The buildings in options A and D would be in exposure B. The building in option C would be in exposure C.

The answer is B.

---

116. Which of the following is used to classify tornadoes?

    A. Richter scale

    B. Saffir-Simpson scale

    C. modified Mercalli scale

    D. Fujita scale

Solution

The Fujita scale (F-scale) is used to classify tornadoes and their damage. This scale was introduced in 1971 by Tetsuya Theodore Fujita at the University of Chicago. F-0 classifies wind speeds below 73 mph (116 km/h) that result in light damage, while F-5 represents incredible damage and wind speeds from 261 mph to 318 mph (416 km/h to 510 km/h). Though class F-6 exists, winds greater than 318 mph (510 km/h) are unlikely.

An enhanced Fujita scale (EF-Scale) was developed in 2006 to provide additional damage indicators and develop a better correlation between damage and wind speed. In the enhanced Fujita scale, 28 damage indicators (DIs), consisting of buildings, structures, and trees, are defined with different degrees of damage (DODs). Estimates of the wind speeds that will cause the DODs were obtained from a panel of experts.

The National Weather Service has assigned an F-scale rating to each DOD. A correlation was then obtained between F-scale and EF-scale wind speeds using regression analysis. The EF-scale consists of 28 DIs and their corresponding DODs, the expected upper and lower bound wind speed for each DOD, and six EF categories ranging from EF0 to EF5. Category EF0 corresponds to a wind speed range of 65 mph to 85 mph (104.6 km/h to 136.8 km/h), and EF5 to a range of more than 200 mph (more than 321.8 km/h).

The answer is D.

117. The figure below shows a one-story concrete building in plan. Shear walls are placed on all four sides of the building. The lateral wind load acting on the roof diaphragm is 90 lbf/ft (900 N/m). Approximately what is the maximum chord force at the north and south edges of the diaphragm?

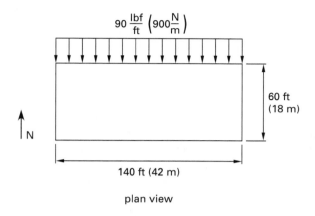

plan view

A.   1600 lbf (4700 N)
B.   3700 lbf (11 000 N)
C.   13,000 lbf (38 000 N)
D.   220,000 lbf (200 000 N)

Solution

The maximum bending moment due to the wind load on the north or south length of the building is

$$M_{max} = \frac{wL^2}{8}$$

w is the uniformly distributed wind load of 90 lbf/ft (900 N/m), and L is the length of the span, 140 ft (42 m).

In U.S. units:

$$M_{max} = \frac{wL^2}{8}$$

$$= \frac{\left(90\,\frac{lbf}{ft}\right)(140\,ft)^2}{8} = 220{,}500\,\text{ft-lbf}$$

In SI units:

$$M_{max} = \frac{wL^2}{8}$$

$$= \frac{\left(900\,\frac{N}{m}\right)(42\,m)^2}{8} = 198\,450\,\text{N·m}$$

A diaphragm system is often compared to the web of an I-shaped girder. The attached walls become, in this case, similar to the flanges of this I-shaped girder. To determine the chord force (F) in the north and south edges of the diaphragm, the maximum bending moment calculated above (M_{max}) must be divided by the width of the diaphragm (d) given here as 60 ft (18 m), which is the arm of this moment.

In U.S. units:

$$F = \frac{M_{max}}{d} = \frac{220{,}500\,\text{ft-lbf}}{60\,\text{ft}}$$

$$= 3675\,\text{lbf}\quad(3700\,\text{lbf})$$

In SI units:

$$F = \frac{M_{max}}{d} = \frac{198\,450\,\text{N·m}}{18\,\text{m}}$$

$$= 11\,025\,\text{N}\quad(11\,000\,\text{N})$$

The answer is B.

118. Which of the following buildings relies on a tuned-mass damper to reduce vibrations due to wind forces?

A.   the International Terminal at San Francisco's International Airport
B.   the Citicorp Building in New York City
C.   the Sears Tower in Chicago
D.   the Petronas Towers in Malaysia

Solution

The building that relies on a tuned-mass damper to reduce vibrations from wind forces is the Citicorp Building in New York City. Its structural engineer William Le Mesurier included in its design a tuned-mass damper, which consists of a heavy mass of concrete sitting in a silicone gel. The mass is synchronized to sway in the opposite direction of the building. When the building moves in one direction, the mass moves in the opposite direction, reducing the building's vibration from wind.

The answer is B.

119. Which of the following statements is FALSE?

    A. The steel skybridge that links the two Petronas Towers in Malaysia connects to the towers with flexible joints, allowing up to 12 in (305) of movement at each end.
    B. In designing the Eiffel Tower, its engineer Gustave Eiffel assumed up to 148 mph (238 km/h) wind at the tower top, which represented winds never encountered in Paris.
    C. The structure of the CN Tower in Toronto sways by about 10 in (254) at the top in a 120 mph (193 km/h) wind.
    D. The structural system of the Statue of Liberty was designed by Gustave Eiffel to sway by about 3 in (76) in a 50 mph (80 km/h) wind.

Solution

The CN Tower in Toronto is so strong that 120 mph (193 km/h) winds would barely create a wobble at the tower top. The CN Tower is the tallest freestanding structure in the world at 1815 ft (553 m). It was completed in 1975 at a cost of $57 million, and built by Canadian National Railways as a way of improving television reception in the area. It was constructed using prestressed concrete and a special construction technique. High-quality concrete was poured into a massive mold, called a *slip form*, and as the concrete hardened, this slip form was raised by a ring of hydraulic jacks. The tower rose about 20 ft (6 m) a day using this technique.

The cross section of the tower base has the shape of the letter Y. This base has three equal legs that are hollow at their ends. At the leg's junction, three compartments house two elevators and a metal staircase. The second part of the tower is called the skypod. It consists of a seven-story structure that is suspended in the air and wrapped around the tower like a doughnut. The third part of the tower is the space deck, which offers spectacular views to visitors. It is supported by cantilevers from the concrete tower top. The transmission mast at the top of the tower is 335 ft (102 m) long. A helicopter mounted this mast by airlifting its 39 sections into place.

The answer is C.

NOTABLE STRUCTURES AND ENGINEERS

120. The first cable roof buildings in the United States date back to the

    A. 1910s and 1920s
    B. 1930s and 1940s
    C. 1950s and 1960s
    D. 1980s

Solution

The first cable roof buildings in the United States date back to the 1950s and 1960s. The North Carolina State Fair Building in Raleigh is considered the first major cable roof building in the United States. It was designed by architects Matthew Nowicki and William Henley Deitrick, and was completed in 1953. It has a 300 ft (91 m) diameter cable structure. Other examples of the early cable roof buildings in the United States are the Villita Assembly Hall in San Antonio, built in 1960; the Automobile Museum Building in Petit Jean Mountain, Arkansas, built in 1964; and the Pan American Terminal at JFK Airport in New York City, built in 1959.

The answer is C.

121. What structural material was used by Pier Luigi Nervi in the design and construction of the dome of the Palazzetto dello Sport arena in Rome?

    A. steel
    B. timber
    C. regular reinforced concrete
    D. prestressed concrete

Solution

The dome of the Palazzetto dello Sport designed by Nervi was erected using prefabricated units of prestressed concrete. It consists of a huge dome carried on obliquely placed Y-shaped legs. It was built between 1956 and 1958 as part of the Rome Olympic Games Complex.

The answer is D.

122. The CBS Building in New York City is an example of

    A. a typical steel-framed skyscraper

    B. a skyscraper with a reinforced concrete frame

    C. a skyscraper with heavy loadbearing masonry walls

    D. the tubular design concept

Solution

The CBS Building in New York City is an example of a skyscraper with a reinforced concrete frame. It was designed by Eero Saarinen and engineered by Weidlinger Associates. Reinforced concrete is generally lagging behind steel in skyscraper construction, so most skyscrapers are built using steel. However, as concrete strength increases, an increasing number of skyscrapers are built using reinforced concrete.

The answer is B.

123. What is the main structural material used to build the Fuller Building (also known as the Flatiron Building) in New York City?

    A. steel

    B. reinforced concrete

    C. load-bearing masonry walls

    D. precast concrete

Solution

The structural material used to build the Fuller, or Flatiron, Building in New York City is steel. The Fuller Building is considered the first skyscraper in New York City. Built in 1902, it has 22 stories and a height of 285 ft (87 m). It was designed by architect Daniel Burnham, and was nicknamed "Flatiron" because of its striking shape resembling the tip of an ocean liner. Its shape was dictated by its triangular site.

Early skyscrapers were generally built with heavy load-bearing masonry walls. The thickness of these walls kept getting larger as buildings got taller, until engineer/architect William Le Baron Jenney invented the concept of the steel frame to carry the loads in a building. Designer Daniel Burnham used that steel frame concept in the Fuller Building. The walls are made of limestone and terracotta and are non-load-bearing. It was built by a prominent construction company, George A. Fuller. The Fuller Company moved out of the building in 1929 and the building was added to the National Register of Historic Places in 1979.

The answer is A.

124. Who was the structural engineer for the Petronas Towers in Malaysia?

    A. Leslie Robertson

    B. Ove Arup & Partners

    C. Thornton-Tomasetti

    D. Weidlinger Associates

Solution

The structural engineer for the Petronas Towers in Malaysia was the firm of Thornton-Tomasetti. The towers were named the world's tallest buildings in 1996. Prior to their construction, the title was held by the Sears Tower in Chicago. The Petronas Towers were designed by architect Cesar Pelli, and consist of a twin tower structure with a height of 1483 ft (452 m). The towers are the headquarters of Petroleum National Berhad, a government-owned oil company. They are built using mainly reinforced concrete. Steel is used for the concrete-filled metal decks, and as framing for the skybridge that connects the two towers. This bridge is double-decked and it spans about 190 ft (58 m).

The answer is C.

125. The ancient dome of Hagia Sophia suffered some collapses during its history. What is believed to be the reason for these collapses?

    A. excessively long spans

    B. inadequate building materials

    C. excessive height

    D. earthquakes

Solution

Earthquakes are believed to be the reason for the collapses of the Hagia Sophia dome. Hagia Sophia was the world's largest church for nine centuries. It was built in Constantinople under the Byzantine Empire and the Emperor Justinian, and was completed in A.D. 537. It consists of a brick dome perched atop four great limestone piers.

It is basically a round dome on top of a rectangular base of 220 ft by 300 ft (67 m by 91 m). The piers support four giant brick arches that transfer the loads from the dome to the piers. Half-domes were added behind the arches at the east and west to help absorb the lateral thrust, thus providing more support to the central dome. Buttresses were also built to the north and south of the church. Substantial deformations of the piers occurred before the arches were completed. As a result, the architects strengthened the buttresses outside the church's north and south walls. Despite

these efforts, the dome collapsed in A.D. 558 after two
earthquakes. It was replaced by a higher dome, which also
suffered some partial collapses after some earthquakes.

The answer is D.

STRUCTURAL LAYOUT VIGNETTE

Directions

Create a two-level roof framing solution based on the given floor plan and program requirements. The layout you design should be structurally sound and efficient.

Your layout should show the location of columns and/or load-bearing walls, the placement of beams, and the placement and spacing of roof joists. You may not add walls. All walls are assumed to be non-load-bearing unless you designate them otherwise. Indicate the span direction of decking. (On the actual exam, the software will include tools to designate load-bearing walls and indicate span direction.)

Program

The preliminary floor plan for a bookstore is given and you are required to develop a roof framing layout for this building. The layout must accommodate the conditions and requirements given below.

Site and Foundation

1. The site has no seismic or wind pressure requirements.

2. The soils and foundation system are adequate for normal loads.

3. Concentrated and special loads need not be considered.

Construction and Materials

1. A steel structural system consisting of open web joists has been chosen for the roof structure.

2. Steel beam sections are to be rolled.

3. The metal deck on the joists is capable of carrying design loads on spans up to and including 4 ft (1220).

4. Joists are sized to carry roof loads only.

General Requirements

1. All roof framing is flat.

2. Cantilevers should not be used.

3. Columns may be located within walls, including window walls and the clerestory window wall.

4. Walls on the floor plan may be designated as bearing walls. Additional bearing walls are not allowed.

5. Lintels must be shown at all openings in bearing walls.

6. The area designated for books must be free of columns.

7. The openings located between the area designated for books and the area designated for music and entertainment must be free of columns.

8. The glazed opening between the area designated for books and the area designated for music and entertainment must be free of columns.

9. Window walls extend to the underside of the structure above.

10. The roof over the area designated for books must be higher than the roof over the remaining area. The roof over the area designated for books is 16 ft (4880) above the floor. The roof over the remaining areas is 12 ft (3660) above the floor.

11. The structure must accommodate a clerestory window to be located along the full length of the east wall of the area designated for books.

Tips

*   On the actual exam, draw the structural elements for the lower roof framing first. Then switch layers and draw the additional structural elements required for the upper roof framing. To be scored, the solution must be drawn on the two separate layers.

*   To select an element overlapped by other elements, keep clicking without moving the mouse until the desired element is highlighted.

Warnings

*   On the actual exam, the *draw joists* tool works like a two-point rectangle and allows the direction and spacing of joists to be selected. Do not draw individual joists.

*   On the actual exam, the *draw decking* tool also works like a two-point rectangle and allows the direction of the joists to be selected.

Tools

Useful tools include the following.

*   *zoom* tool for checking the location of elements

*   full-screen cursor to help line up structural elements

Target Time: 1 hour

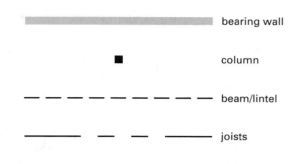

bearing wall

column

beam/lintel

joists

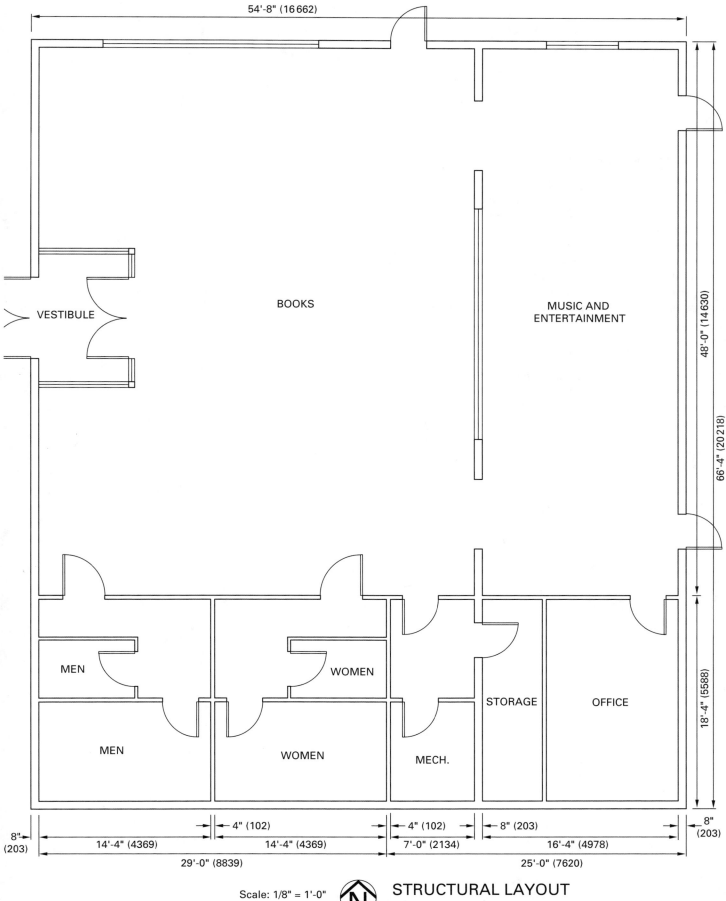

54'-8" (16 662)

48'-0" (14 630)

66'-4" (20 218)

VESTIBULE

BOOKS

MUSIC AND
ENTERTAINMENT

18'-4" (5588)

MEN

MEN

WOMEN

WOMEN

MECH.

STORAGE

OFFICE

8"
(203)

8"
(203)

4" (102)

4" (102)

8" (203)

14'-4" (4369)

14'-4" (4369)

7'-0" (2134)

16'-4" (4978)

29'-0" (8839)

25'-0" (7620)

Scale: 1/8" = 1'-0"
(1:100 metric)

STRUCTURAL LAYOUT

STRUCTURAL LAYOUT: PASSING SOLUTION

This vignette requires the candidate to lay out a basic structural concept for a small building by placing columns, bearing walls, steel joists, and decking. The problem includes a building with two different roof heights and various types of openings.

Lower Roof Framing

The lower roof is supported on steel joists and metal decking. The joist spacing at 4 ft (1220) on center is within the program limits. The three long north-south walls are designated as load-bearing walls, and the joists are spanning perpendicular to these walls and are supported mainly on them. The east-west walls at the edges of the lower roof area need not be load-bearing. Joists drawn at these edges compensate for the lack of load-bearing walls there. Lintels are provided at all doorways and window openings in the load-bearing walls.

Upper Roof Framing

The upper roof area is supported on steel joists and metal decking as well. Again, joist spacing at 4 ft (1220) on center is within the limits of the program. The four columns shown are supported on the load-bearing walls. The steel beams supported on these columns accommodate the clerestory window located along the full length of the east wall of the area for books.

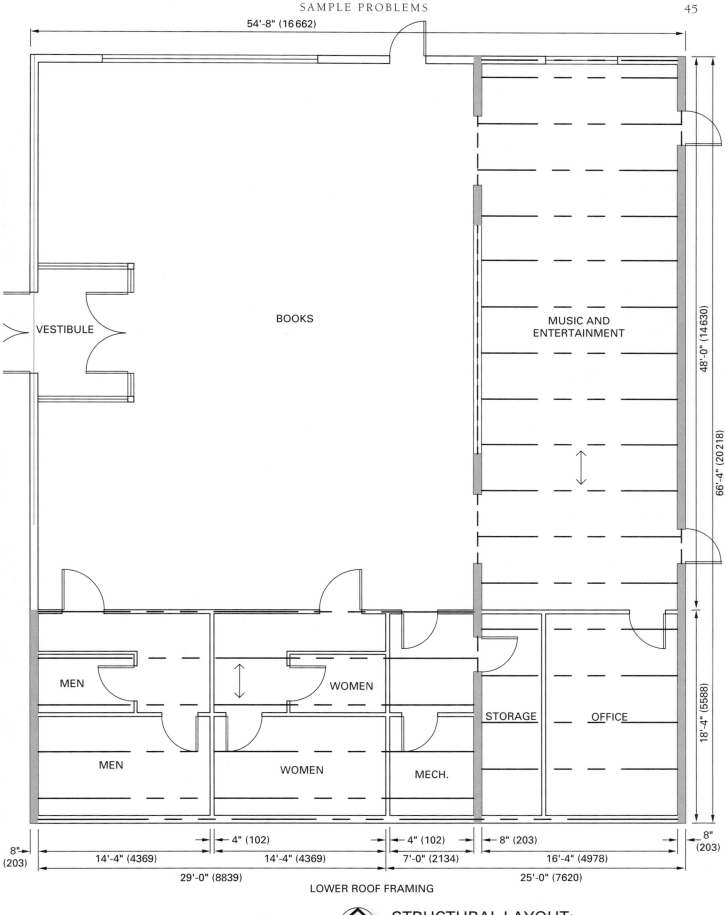

54'-8" (16 662)

VESTIBULE

BOOKS

MUSIC AND
ENTERTAINMENT

48'-0" (14 630)

66'-4" (20 218)

MEN

MEN

WOMEN

WOMEN

MECH.

STORAGE

OFFICE

18'-4" (5588)

8"
(203)

4" (102)

4" (102)

8" (203)

8"
(203)

14'-4" (4369)

14'-4" (4369)

7'-0" (2134)

16'-4" (4978)

29'-0" (8839)

25'-0" (7620)

LOWER ROOF FRAMING

Scale: 1/8" = 1'-0"
(1:100 metric)

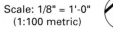

STRUCTURAL LAYOUT:
PASSING SOLUTION

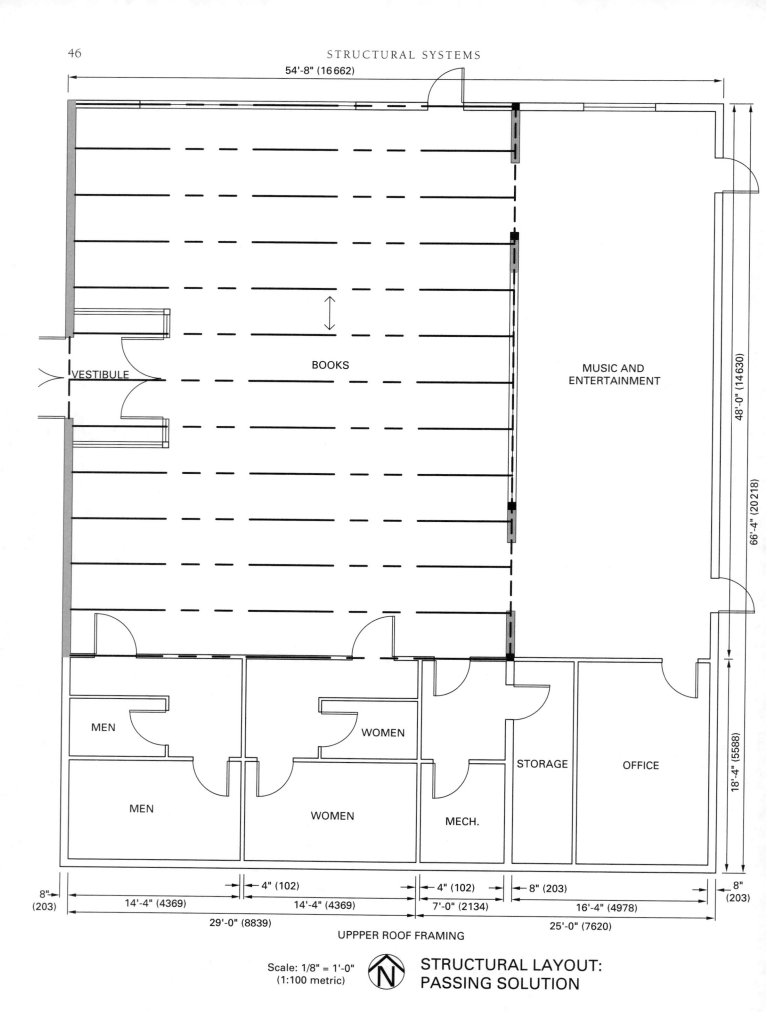

54'-8" (16 662)

48'-0" (14 630)

66'-4" (20 218)

18'-4" (5588)

VESTIBULE

BOOKS

MUSIC AND
ENTERTAINMENT

MEN

MEN

WOMEN

WOMEN

MECH.

STORAGE

OFFICE

8"
(203)

14'-4" (4369)

4" (102)

14'-4" (4369)

4" (102)

7'-0" (2134)

8" (203)

16'-4" (4978)

8"
(203)

29'-0" (8839)

25'-0" (7620)

UPPPER ROOF FRAMING

Scale: 1/8" = 1'-0"
(1:100 metric)

N

STRUCTURAL LAYOUT:
PASSING SOLUTION

STRUCTURAL LAYOUT: FAILING SOLUTION

Lower Roof Framing

The framing suggested in this solution is unacceptable for various reasons. The joist spacing drawn at 5 ft (1524) on center exceeds the limits of the program. The north-south walls are designated as load-bearing, but the intermediate wall at the north edge of the office and storage area is not. Instead, only two columns are placed at the east and west ends of this wall, forcing the beam to span over 54 ft (16.5 m). The joist at the west edge of the music and entertainment area seems to be supported on this 54 ft (16.5 m) long beam as well.

Upper Roof Solution

Again, the joist spacing drawn at 5 ft (1525) on center exceeds the limits of the program. The wall at the south edge of the area for books is not load-bearing. Instead, joists are supported on a beam which in turn is supported on two columns at its ends. However, the column referred to as Column A on this framing plan is not shown on the lower roof framing, suggesting that it is not continuous to the foundation. Column A seems to be supported instead on the 54 ft (16.5 m) long beam discussed above, adding even more load on that beam, and making the structural layout even less acceptable.

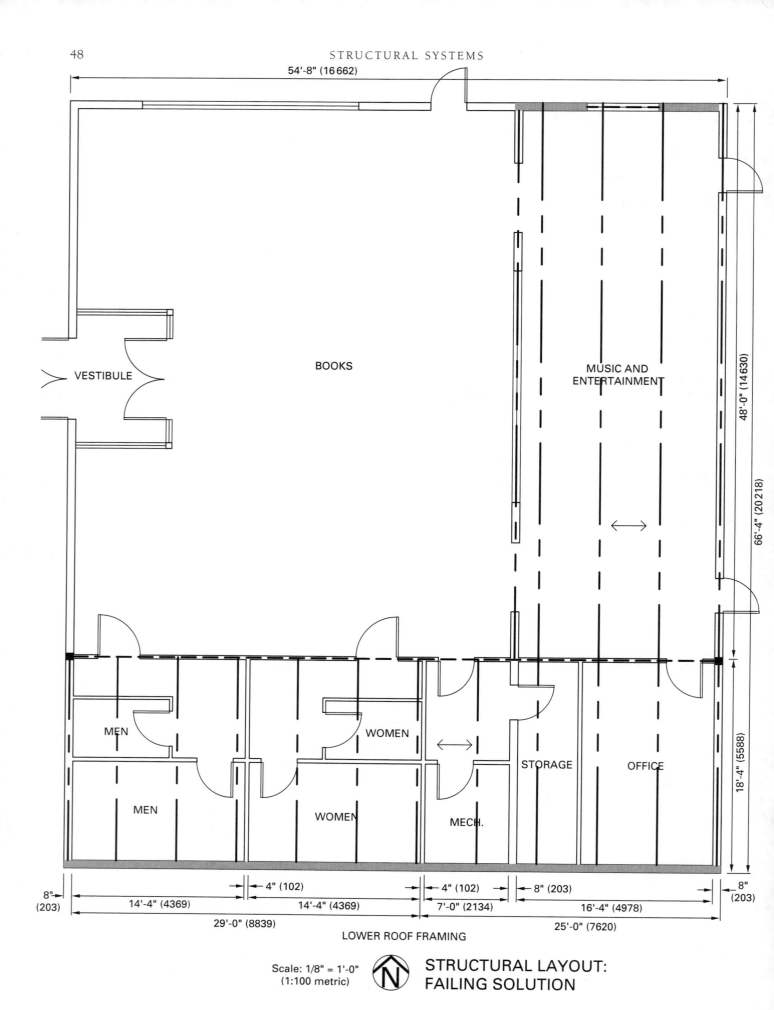

54'-8" (16 662)

VESTIBULE

BOOKS

MUSIC AND
ENTERTAINMENT

48'-0" (14 630)

66'-4" (20 218)

MEN

MEN

WOMEN

WOMEN

MECH.

STORAGE

OFFICE

18'-4" (5588)

8"
(203)

14'-4" (4369)

4" (102)

14'-4" (4369)

4" (102)

7'-0" (2134)

8" (203)

16'-4" (4978)

8"
(203)

29'-0" (8839)

25'-0" (7620)

LOWER ROOF FRAMING

Scale: 1/8" = 1'-0"
(1:100 metric)

STRUCTURAL LAYOUT:
FAILING SOLUTION

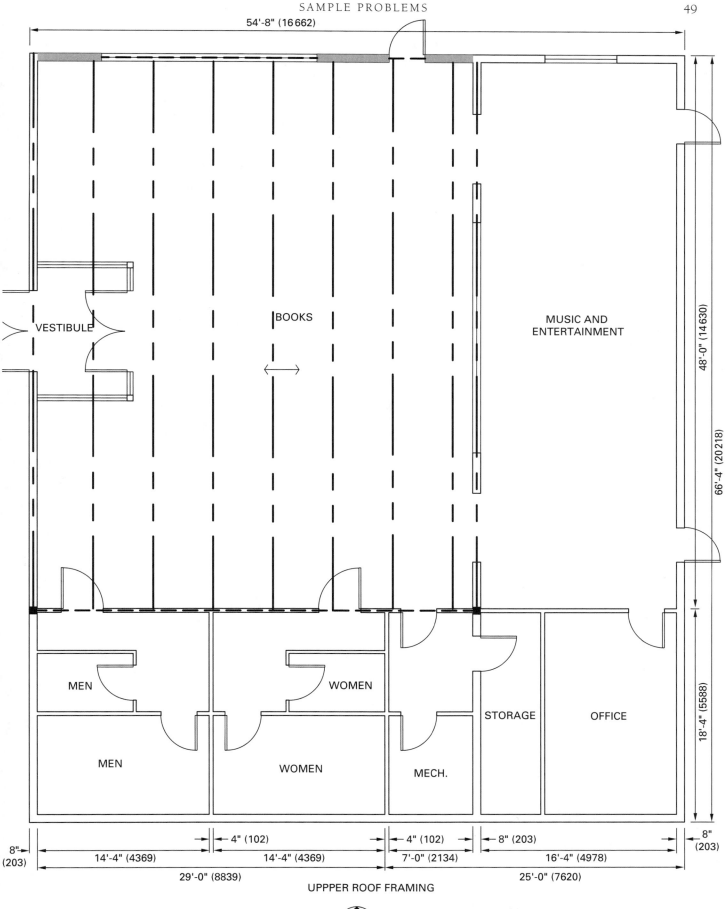

54'-8" (16 662)

48'-0" (14 630)

66'-4" (20 218)

18'-4" (5588)

VESTIBULE

BOOKS

MUSIC AND
ENTERTAINMENT

MEN

WOMEN

STORAGE

OFFICE

MEN

WOMEN

MECH.

8"
(203)

4" (102)

4" (102)

8" (203)

8"
(203)

14'-4" (4369)

14'-4" (4369)

7'-0" (2134)

16'-4" (4978)

29'-0" (8839)

25'-0" (7620)

UPPPER ROOF FRAMING

Scale: 1/8" = 1'-0"
(1:100 metric)

STRUCTURAL LAYOUT:
FAILING SOLUTION

PRACTICE EXAM: MULTIPLE CHOICE

Directions

Reference books should not be used on this practice exam. Besides this book, you should have only a calculator, pencils, and scratch paper. (On the actual exam, these will be provided and should not be brought into the site.)

Target Time: 1.5 hours

1. Ⓐ Ⓑ Ⓒ Ⓓ	26. Ⓐ Ⓑ Ⓒ Ⓓ	51. Ⓐ Ⓑ Ⓒ Ⓓ
2. Ⓐ Ⓑ Ⓒ Ⓓ	27. Ⓐ Ⓑ Ⓒ Ⓓ	52. Ⓐ Ⓑ Ⓒ Ⓓ
3. Ⓐ Ⓑ Ⓒ Ⓓ	28. Ⓐ Ⓑ Ⓒ Ⓓ	53. Ⓐ Ⓑ Ⓒ Ⓓ
4. Ⓐ Ⓑ Ⓒ Ⓓ	29. Ⓐ Ⓑ Ⓒ Ⓓ	54. Ⓐ Ⓑ Ⓒ Ⓓ
5. Ⓐ Ⓑ Ⓒ Ⓓ	30. Ⓐ Ⓑ Ⓒ Ⓓ	55. Ⓐ Ⓑ Ⓒ Ⓓ
6. Ⓐ Ⓑ Ⓒ Ⓓ	31. Ⓐ Ⓑ Ⓒ Ⓓ	56. Ⓐ Ⓑ Ⓒ Ⓓ
7. Ⓐ Ⓑ Ⓒ Ⓓ	32. Ⓐ Ⓑ Ⓒ Ⓓ	57. Ⓐ Ⓑ Ⓒ Ⓓ
8. Ⓐ Ⓑ Ⓒ Ⓓ	33. Ⓐ Ⓑ Ⓒ Ⓓ	58. Ⓐ Ⓑ Ⓒ Ⓓ
9. Ⓐ Ⓑ Ⓒ Ⓓ	34. Ⓐ Ⓑ Ⓒ Ⓓ	59. Ⓐ Ⓑ Ⓒ Ⓓ
10. Ⓐ Ⓑ Ⓒ Ⓓ	35. _____	60. Ⓐ Ⓑ Ⓒ Ⓓ
11. Ⓐ Ⓑ Ⓒ Ⓓ	36. Ⓐ Ⓑ Ⓒ Ⓓ	61. Ⓐ Ⓑ Ⓒ Ⓓ
12. Ⓐ Ⓑ Ⓒ Ⓓ Ⓔ Ⓕ	37. Ⓐ Ⓑ Ⓒ Ⓓ	62. Ⓐ Ⓑ Ⓒ Ⓓ
13. Ⓐ Ⓑ Ⓒ Ⓓ	38. _____	63. Ⓐ Ⓑ Ⓒ Ⓓ
14. Ⓐ Ⓑ Ⓒ Ⓓ	39. Ⓐ Ⓑ Ⓒ Ⓓ	64. Ⓐ Ⓑ Ⓒ Ⓓ
15. Ⓐ Ⓑ Ⓒ Ⓓ	40. Ⓐ Ⓑ Ⓒ Ⓓ	65. Ⓐ Ⓑ Ⓒ Ⓓ
16. Ⓐ Ⓑ Ⓒ Ⓓ	41. Ⓐ Ⓑ Ⓒ Ⓓ	66. Ⓐ Ⓑ Ⓒ Ⓓ
17. Ⓐ Ⓑ Ⓒ Ⓓ	42. Ⓐ Ⓑ Ⓒ Ⓓ	67. Ⓐ Ⓑ Ⓒ Ⓓ
18. Ⓐ Ⓑ Ⓒ Ⓓ Ⓔ Ⓕ	43. Ⓐ Ⓑ Ⓒ Ⓓ	68. Ⓐ Ⓑ Ⓒ Ⓓ
19. Ⓐ Ⓑ Ⓒ Ⓓ Ⓔ Ⓕ	44. Ⓐ Ⓑ Ⓒ Ⓓ	69. Ⓐ Ⓑ Ⓒ Ⓓ
20. Ⓐ Ⓑ Ⓒ Ⓓ	45. Ⓐ Ⓑ Ⓒ Ⓓ	70. Ⓐ Ⓑ Ⓒ Ⓓ
21. Ⓐ Ⓑ Ⓒ Ⓓ	46. Ⓐ Ⓑ Ⓒ Ⓓ	71. Ⓐ Ⓑ Ⓒ Ⓓ
22. Ⓐ Ⓑ Ⓒ Ⓓ Ⓔ Ⓕ	47. Ⓐ Ⓑ Ⓒ Ⓓ	72. Ⓐ Ⓑ Ⓒ Ⓓ
23. Ⓐ Ⓑ Ⓒ Ⓓ	48. Ⓐ Ⓑ Ⓒ Ⓓ	73. Ⓐ Ⓑ Ⓒ Ⓓ
24. Ⓐ Ⓑ Ⓒ Ⓓ Ⓔ Ⓕ	49. Ⓐ Ⓑ Ⓒ Ⓓ	74. Ⓐ Ⓑ Ⓒ Ⓓ
25. Ⓐ Ⓑ Ⓒ Ⓓ	50. Ⓐ Ⓑ Ⓒ Ⓓ	75. Ⓐ Ⓑ Ⓒ Ⓓ

76. Ⓐ Ⓑ Ⓒ Ⓓ
77. Ⓐ Ⓑ Ⓒ Ⓓ
78. Ⓐ Ⓑ Ⓒ Ⓓ Ⓔ Ⓕ
79. Ⓐ Ⓑ Ⓒ Ⓓ
80. Ⓐ Ⓑ Ⓒ Ⓓ
81. Ⓐ Ⓑ Ⓒ Ⓓ Ⓔ Ⓕ
82. Ⓐ Ⓑ Ⓒ Ⓓ
83. Ⓐ Ⓑ Ⓒ Ⓓ
84. Ⓐ Ⓑ Ⓒ Ⓓ
85. Ⓐ Ⓑ Ⓒ Ⓓ
86. Ⓐ Ⓑ Ⓒ Ⓓ
87. Ⓐ Ⓑ Ⓒ Ⓓ
88. Ⓐ Ⓑ Ⓒ Ⓓ
89. Ⓐ Ⓑ Ⓒ Ⓓ
90. Ⓐ Ⓑ Ⓒ Ⓓ
91. Ⓐ Ⓑ Ⓒ Ⓓ
92. Ⓐ Ⓑ Ⓒ Ⓓ

93. Ⓐ Ⓑ Ⓒ Ⓓ
94. Ⓐ Ⓑ Ⓒ Ⓓ
95. Ⓐ Ⓑ Ⓒ Ⓓ
96. Ⓐ Ⓑ Ⓒ Ⓓ
97. Ⓐ Ⓑ Ⓒ Ⓓ
98. Ⓐ Ⓑ Ⓒ Ⓓ
99. Ⓐ Ⓑ Ⓒ Ⓓ
100. Ⓐ Ⓑ Ⓒ Ⓓ
101. Ⓐ Ⓑ Ⓒ Ⓓ
102. Ⓐ Ⓑ Ⓒ Ⓓ
103. Ⓐ Ⓑ Ⓒ Ⓓ
104. Ⓐ Ⓑ Ⓒ Ⓓ
105. Ⓐ Ⓑ Ⓒ Ⓓ
106. Ⓐ Ⓑ Ⓒ Ⓓ
107. Ⓐ Ⓑ Ⓒ Ⓓ
108. Ⓐ Ⓑ Ⓒ Ⓓ
109. Ⓐ Ⓑ Ⓒ Ⓓ

110. _____
111. Ⓐ Ⓑ Ⓒ Ⓓ
112. Ⓐ Ⓑ Ⓒ Ⓓ
113. Ⓐ Ⓑ Ⓒ Ⓓ
114. Ⓐ Ⓑ Ⓒ Ⓓ
115. Ⓐ Ⓑ Ⓒ Ⓓ
116. Ⓐ Ⓑ Ⓒ Ⓓ
117. Ⓐ Ⓑ Ⓒ Ⓓ
118. Ⓐ Ⓑ Ⓒ Ⓓ
119. Ⓐ Ⓑ Ⓒ Ⓓ
120. Ⓐ Ⓑ Ⓒ Ⓓ
121. Ⓐ Ⓑ Ⓒ Ⓓ
122. Ⓐ Ⓑ Ⓒ Ⓓ
123. _____
124. Ⓐ Ⓑ Ⓒ Ⓓ
125. Ⓐ Ⓑ Ⓒ Ⓓ

1. A force of 100 lbf (100 N) is resolved into two components at 40° and 80° angles with the force.

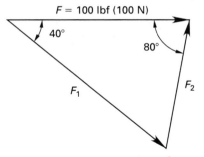

These two components are approximately

- A. 11 lbf and 7.4 lbf (11 N and 7.4 N)
- B. 110 lbf and 74 lbf (110 N and 74 N)
- C. 230 lbf and 150 lbf (230 N and 150 N)
- D. 300 lbf and 200 lbf (300 N and 200 N)

2. Compared to hurricanes, tornadoes generally

- A. are smaller in diameter and have faster wind speeds
- B. are larger in diameter and have faster wind speeds
- C. are smaller in diameter and have slower wind speeds
- D. are larger in diameter and have slower wind speeds

3. A simply supported beam carries a concentrated load of 7000 lbf (4000 N) as shown. Neglect the beam weight.

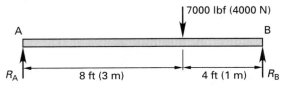

The support reactions (R_A and R_B) of the beam are approximately

- A. 23 lbf and 47 lbf (100 N and 300 N)
- B. 2000 lbf and 5000 lbf (1500 N and 2500 N)
- C. 2300 lbf and 4700 lbf (1000 N and 3000 N)
- D. 3500 lbf and 3500 lbf (2000 N and 2000 N)

4. In order to compare wind measurements from different wind stations, wind is measured at a standard height above the ground surface. What is that height?

- A. 3 ft (0.9 m)
- B. 10 ft (3.0 m)
- C. 25 ft (7.6 m)
- D. 33 ft (10.0 m)

5. Stress in a body is

- A. an internal resistance to deformation
- B. the change in size due to force
- C. the tendency of the body to rotate
- D. all of the above

6. What type of wind pressure do the windward and leeward walls of a building receive?

- A. suction (negative) pressure on the windward wall and direct (positive) pressure on the leeward wall
- B. direct (positive) pressure on the windward wall and suction (negative) pressure on the leeward wall
- C. suction (negative) pressure on both walls
- D. direct (positive) pressure on both walls

7. A steel rod has a diameter of 2 in (50) and a length of 10 ft (3 m). The rod is subjected to a tension force of 10,000 lbf (5000 N). What is the approximate tension stress in the rod?

- A. 320 psi (0.26 MPa)
- B. 400 psi (0.30 MPa)
- C. 3200 psi (2.6 MPa)
- D. 4000 psi (3.0 MPa)

8. Corners and eaves are generally

- A. subject to higher wind forces
- B. subject to lower wind forces
- C. subject to the same amount of wind forces as the rest of the building
- D. not affected by wind forces

9. 40 ft (10 m) long precast concrete paving slabs are to be placed at 55°F (15°C). Approximately how wide should the gap be between the slabs so that they will touch each other at 85°F (30°C)? The coefficient of linear expansion of concrete is 5.5×10^{-6} in/in-°F (9.9×10^{-6} mm/mm·°C).

A. 0.079 in (1.5)
B. 0.40 in (7.0)
C. 0.79 in (15)
D. 4.0 in (70)

10. The direct wind pressure on a vertical surface is

A. directly proportional to the wind velocity
B. inversely proportional to the wind velocity
C. directly proportional to the square of the wind velocity
D. not related to the wind velocity

11. A positive bending moment at a section of a beam implies

A. compression stress in the top fibers of the beam and tension stress in the bottom fibers
B. tension stress in the top fibers of the beam and compression stress in the bottom fibers
C. compression stress in all fibers of the section
D. that the bending moment is not related to tension and compression stresses

12. Which of the following factors affect the wind pressure on a building? (Choose the four that apply.)

A. wind speed
B. terrain surrounding the building
C. soil type
D. building height
E. building weight
F. building shape

13. A rectangular cross section has a width of 5 in (120) and a depth of 8 in (200). What is the approximate moment of inertia of this cross section about the horizontal centroidal axis AB?

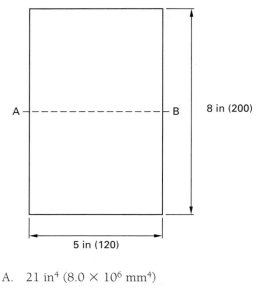

A. 21 in⁴ (8.0×10^6 mm⁴)
B. 83 in⁴ (3.2×10^7 mm⁴)
C. 160 in⁴ (6.1×10^7 mm⁴)
D. 210 in⁴ (8.0×10^7 mm⁴)

14. In a simply supported beam, where does the shear force take its maximum value?

A. at the center of the span
B. at a support
C. at one-third of the span
D. depends on the loads and could be at a support or at a point along the span

15. The effect of which of the following events is NOT covered in building codes?

A. hurricane
B. tornado
C. earthquake
D. snow

16. What is the most widely used structural steel in buildings?

A. A36
B. A242
C. A514
D. A588

17.   A building's lateral displacement due to wind forces is called

   A.   drift
   B.   the P-delta effect
   C.   torsion
   D.   pounding

18.   When designing a beam, why is it necessary to control deflection? (Choose the four that apply.)

   A.   Excessive deflection is visually disturbing.
   B.   Excessive deflection can break adjacent windows.
   C.   Excessive deflection is a sign that the beam is unsafe in bending.
   D.   Excessive deflection is a sign that the beam is unsafe in shear.
   E.   Excessive deflection can crack adjacent partitions.
   F.   Excessive deflection can crack adjacent plaster ceilings.

19.   What are the reasons for limiting drift? (Choose the two that apply.)

   A.   Drift leads to base shear.
   B.   Drift is the main cause of torsion.
   C.   Drift is visually disturbing.
   D.   Drift can cause damage to the brittle elements in a building.
   E.   Drift can affect the comfort of a building's occupants.
   F.   Drift creates an overturning moment.

20.   The deflection of a steel beam is related to

I.   the load applied on the beam
II.   the length of the span
III.   the yield stress of the steel
IV.   the moment of inertia of the section

   A.   I and II only
   B.   III and IV only
   C.   I, II, and III only
   D.   I, II, and IV only

21.   The maps of basic wind speeds given by the IBC and by ASCE/SEI 7 *Minimum Design Loads for Buildings and Other Structures* both mention some special wind regions. These are regions

   A.   where the basic wind speed is negligible
   B.   where the basic wind speed is less than 70 mph (113 km/h)
   C.   where the basic wind speed is higher than 140 mph (225 km/h)
   D.   that are excluded from the map and for which wind speeds must be determined from local records

22.   Which of the following can prevent the lateral buckling of steel beams? (Choose the three that apply.)

   A.   encasing the tension flange in concrete
   B.   encasing the compression flange in concrete
   C.   fully encasing the beam in concrete
   D.   welding the metal decking to the top flange
   E.   using only wide-flange shapes
   F.   providing intermediate lateral support or bracing every 10 ft

23.   What is the value of the gradient height for urban or metropolitan areas?

   A.   900 ft (270 m)
   B.   1200 ft (370 m)
   C.   1500 ft (460 m)
   D.   2000 ft (610 m)

24.   In the wind design method outlined in ASCE/SEI 7, what are the elements considered when using factor K_z? (Choose the three that apply.)

   A.   building height
   B.   building weight
   C.   building orientation
   D.   exposure
   E.   wind gusting
   F.   occupancy type

25. The tendency of a column to buckle increases with

I.   an increase in the length
II. a decrease in the length
III. an increase in the radius of gyration
IV. a decrease in the radius of gyration

   A. I and III only
   B. I and IV only
   C. II and III only
   D. II and IV only

26. The risk of overturning due to wind force is

   A. higher in buildings with a high height-to-width ratio
   B. lower in buildings with a high height-to-width ratio
   C. higher in buildings with a low height-to-width ratio
   D. lower in top-heavy buildings than bottom- or base-heavy buildings

27. Neglecting the beam weight, what is the shape of the shear diagram for the simple beam loaded as shown?

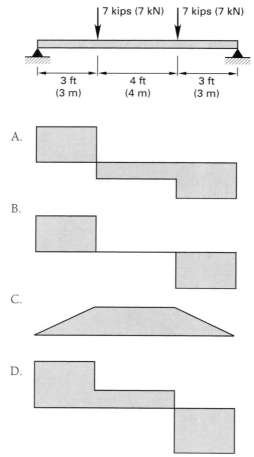

28. A steel beam is simply supported over a span of 20 ft. It carries a uniformly distributed load of 3000 lbf/ft, including an allowance for the beam weight. The steel is ASTM A36, and the allowable bending stress is $F_b = 0.66F_y$. Use Table 11, Allowable Stress Design Selection, in the Appendix. What is the most economical and safe size for this beam?

   A. W12 × 72
   B. W14 × 53
   C. W21 × 44
   D. W21 × 50

29. The moment-resisting frame is an appropriate system to use for resisting wind forces in

   A. low-rise buildings only
   B. low-rise buildings and high-rise buildings of 30 stories or less
   C. high-rise buildings of approximately 50 stories
   D. high-rise buildings of any height

30. Which of the following shapes can be used for steel columns?

I.   structural tees
II. W shapes
III. structural tubing
IV. W shapes that are reinforced with flange plates

   A. II only
   B. I and II only
   C. II and III only
   D. II, III, and IV only

31. A small, one-story commercial building with a total height of 14 ft (4.3 m) is to be built on a flat site in the downtown area of San Francisco. The building is to have a flat roof and a rectangular floor plan of 40 ft by 20 ft (12 m by 6 m). Use Fig. 1, Basic Wind Speed, and Table 12, Velocity Pressure Exposure Coefficients, in the Appendix. The formula for the basic wind velocity pressure is

$$q = 0.00256K_zK_{zt}K_dv^2I \quad \text{[U.S. units]}$$

$$q = 0.613K_zK_{zt}K_dv^2I \quad \text{[SI units]}$$

Using Method 2 from ASCE/SEI 7, what is approximately the basic wind velocity pressure?

   A. 4.1 psf (200 N/m²)
   B. 6.1 psf (290 N/m²)
   C. 9.0 psf (430 N/m²)
   D. 10 psf (490 N/m²)

32. Neglecting the beam weight, what is the general shape of the bending moment diagram for the cantilever beam loaded as shown?

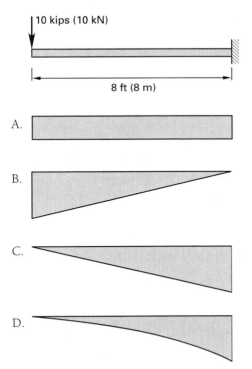

33. According to Fig. 1, Basic Wind Speed, in the Appendix, what is the basic wind speed in San Francisco?

    A. 85 mph (38 m/s)

    B. 90 mph (40 m/s)

    C. 100 mph (45 m/s)

    D. San Francisco is located in a special wind region.

34. A three-story braced frame is subjected to lateral forces and dead loads as shown. What is most nearly the overturning moment at the base of the frame?

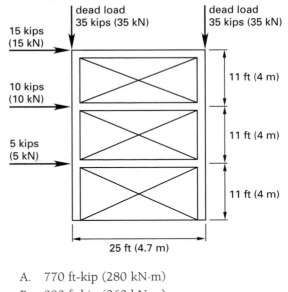

    A. 770 ft-kip (280 kN·m)

    B. 990 ft-kip (360 kN·m)

    C. 1650 ft-kip (550 kN·m)

    D. 2500 ft-kip (810 kN·m)

35. A column of ASTM A36 steel has an unbraced height of 11 ft and carries an axial load of 200 kips, including its own weight. K equals 1 for both axes. Use Table 13, Columns: W Shapes, in the Appendix. The safe, economical W-shape section for this column is W14 × ____. (Fill in the blank.)

36. Which of the following statements about glulam members is FALSE?

    A. Structural properties of glulam members generally exceed those of sawn lumber.

    B. Glulam beams can only be used with short spans and light loads.

    C. Glulam members can sometimes be fabricated using two different kinds of wood, in which case the stronger wood is used for the outer lams, which are subjected to higher stresses.

    D. The general and strong way to use a glulam beam is by having the load applied perpendicular to the wide face of the lams in the plane of beam section or perpendicular to the horizontal centroidal axis.

37. A parapet wall is 3 ft (0.9 m) high and subject to a total wind pressure of 12 psf (600 N/m²). The total design moment for this parapet (per foot of parapet) is approximately

    A. 36 ft-lbf (540 N·m)
    B. 54 ft-lbf (240 N·m)
    C. 110 ft-lbf (480 N·m)
    D. 160 ft-lbf (720 N·m)

38. A sawn lumber floor beam is made of no. 1 douglas-fir larch. The beam is simply supported over a span of 12 ft and is part of a typical floor framing that includes several beams spaced 16 in on centers. The beam carries 27 lbf/ft of dead load and 53 lbf/ft of live load. Assume dry conditions and normal temperature. For no. 1 douglas-fir larch, the allowable bending stress is 1000 psi. Use Table 1, Section Properties of Standard Dressed (S4S) Sawn Lumber, in the Appendix. The size factor is

$C_F = 1.3$ for 2×6
$C_F = 1.2$ for 2×8
$C_F = 1.1$ for 2×10
$C_F = 1.0$ for 2×12

The minimum required safe size in bending for this beam is 2×_____. (Fill in the blank.)

39. How are the diagonal members of the X-bracing of a tall structure normally designed to minimize costs?

    A. One diagonal brace is designed to be stressed in tension while the other is not stressed.
    B. One diagonal brace is designed to be stressed in compression while the other is not stressed.
    C. Both diagonal braces are designed to be stressed in tension at the same time.
    D. Both diagonal braces are designed to be stressed in compression at the same time.

40. Wood I-joists can generally be used for spans

    A. up to about 20 ft (6 m)
    B. up to about 30 ft (9 m)
    C. up to about 45 ft (14 m)
    D. exceeding 100 ft (30 m)

41. In order to resist wind forces, the John Hancock Tower in Chicago was designed using

    A. plain rigid frames
    B. portal framing
    C. trussed tubes
    D. bundled tubes

42. In wood construction, what is the main benefit of using platform framing as opposed to balloon framing?

    A. reduced vertical shrinkage
    B. increased fire resistance
    C. better resistance for lateral loads
    D. ease of construction

43. In order to resist wind forces, the Sears Tower in Chicago was designed using

    A. plain rigid frames
    B. portal framing
    C. trussed tube
    D. bundled tubes

44. Which of the following statements about open-web steel joists is FALSE?

    A. Open-web steel joists can be used for both floor and roof framing.
    B. Open-web steel joists are most commonly used in the case of heavy, concentrated loads.
    C. The lighter the loads and the longer the span, the more economical open-web joists are.
    D. The spacing of open-web joists is generally between 18 in and 8 ft (0.46 m and 2.4 m).

45. Which of the following towers includes in its design a vibration damper in the form of a suspended steel ball?

    A. the John Hancock Tower in Chicago
    B. the Sears Tower in Chicago
    C. the Petronas Towers in Malaysia
    D. Taipei 101 in Taiwan

46. In the open-web steel joists structural system, the deep-long span joists of the DLH-series have depths up to

    A. 30 in (0.76 m)
    B. 4.0 ft (1.2 m)
    C. 6.0 ft (1.8 m)
    D. 10 ft (3.0 m)

47. Roof trusses must generally be designed with

    A. only diagonal bracing in the plane of the top chord
    B. only horizontal lower chord diagonal bracing
    C. only horizontal lower chord straight bracing with continuous struts
    D. diagonal bracing in the plane of the top chords and horizontal straight lower chord bracing with steel struts

48. In wind design, what is the permissible drift of one story relative to an adjacent story in a building where the story height is 12 ft (3.7 m)?

    A. 0.036 in (0.092)
    B. 0.36 in (9.2)
    C. 0.72 in (19)
    D. 1.1 in (28)

49. Which statement is FALSE?

    A. A steel ring is normally placed at the bottom of a steel dome to resist the compression stresses there.
    B. Steel domes have been constructed with diameters exceeding 400 ft (120 m).
    C. A steel dome and bottom ring can be supported on columns spaced around the dome's perimeter.
    D. The steel dome and bottom ring can be supported on bearing walls.

50. Which of the following can be used in the construction of horizontal diaphragms?

    I. plywood
    II. particle board
    III. concrete
    IV. steel decking

    A. I and III only
    B. II and III only
    C. I, II, and IV only
    D. I, II, III, and IV

51. Which statement is FALSE?

    A. In cable-supported roofs, steel cables are used as load-carrying elements that are subject to tension.
    B. In cable-supported roofs, resistance to corrosion is increased by using galvanized wires.
    C. In designing cable roof systems, the forces that require special consideration and attention are primarily the gravity loads.
    D. Compared to traditional systems, cable roof systems are more economical for extremely long spans.

52. Concrete is a construction material that behaves well under

    A. tension
    B. compression
    C. torsion
    D. bending stress

53. Which of these materials CANNOT function as a diaphragm?

    I. straight tongue-and-groove sheathing
    II. light-gauge corrugated metal
    III. concrete
    IV. plywood

    A. I and II only
    B. III and IV only
    C. I, II, and III only
    D. I, II, and IV only

54.   Prestressed concrete is reinforced concrete in which some initial stresses are introduced prior to loading. What is the type of initial stress introduced?

    A. compression stress
    B. tension stress
    C. a combination of compression and tension stresses
    D. shear stress

55.   Which of the following is used to classify hurricanes?

    A. Richter scale
    B. Saffir-Simpson scale
    C. modified Mercalli scale
    D. Fujita scale

56.   Which two of the following scales are used to measure earthquakes?

I.   Richter scale
II.   Saffir-Simpson scale
III. modified Mercalli scale
IV.   Fujita scale

    A. I and II
    B. I and III
    C. I and IV
    D. III and IV

57.   The flat plate concrete deck system is basically a smooth, simple concrete slab supported on

    A. beams on the four sides
    B. a system of beams and girders
    C. columns only
    D. ribs in both directions

58.   In an earthquake, the location deep within the earth where the seismic movement of rock begins is called the

    A. fault
    B. epicenter
    C. hypocenter
    D. tectonic plate

59.   What type of building is best suited for the flat plate concrete deck?

    A. an industrial building
    B. a storage building
    C. an office building
    D. a residential building

60.   What is the benefit of introducing a column capital or a drop panel above the columns in a flat plate system?

    A. to improve aesthetics
    B. to resist the punching shear around the columns
    C. to resist the bending moment in the slab
    D. to reduce the tension in the concrete slab

61.   On the Richter scale, compared to a magnitude 5 earthquake, an earthquake of magnitude 6 releases about

    A. 32 times more energy
    B. 100 times more energy
    C. 1000 times more energy
    D. 32,000 times more energy

62.   A two-way concrete slab is normally reinforced

    A. for bending moment in both directions
    B. for bending moment in the short direction only
    C. for bending moment in the long direction only
    D. only for temperature/shrinkage stresses in both directions

63.   A waffle slab concrete deck system is

    A. ribbed in one direction only
    B. ribbed in both directions
    C. always prestressed
    D. never prestressed

64. Which two of the following statements are correct?

I.   Increasing a building's stiffness increases its fundamental period of vibration.

II. Increasing a building's stiffness decreases its fundamental period of vibration.

III. Increasing a building's mass decreases its fundamental period of vibration.

IV. Increasing a building's mass increases its fundamental period of vibration.

    A. I and III
    B. I and IV
    C. II and III
    D. II and IV

65. What is the function of the stirrups in reinforced concrete beams?

    A. to resist torsion
    B. to resist tension
    C. to resist shear
    D. to resist compression

66. What types of buildings are most suited for a pan joist concrete system?

    A. industrial and storage buildings
    B. residential buildings
    C. hotels
    D. office buildings

67. Prestressed concrete beams may be used for spans with lengths of

    A. no more than 20 ft (6 m)
    B. no more than 40 ft (12 m)
    C. no more than 60 ft (18 m)
    D. 100 ft (30 m) or more

68. Structural systems resist lateral forces by developing

    A. bending
    B. shear
    C. axial tension and compression
    D. bending, shear, or axial tension and compression

69. Which of the following statements about the concrete shell system known as the *dome of revolution* is FALSE?

    A. The dome of revolution is a segment of a sphere.
    B. Most stresses in the dome of revolution are bending stresses.
    C. The dome of revolution is generally supported on columns or a load-bearing wall.
    D. The dome of revolution often has acoustical problems that may be difficult to resolve.

70. Moment-resisting frames generally resist lateral forces by developing

    A. bending
    B. shear
    C. tension
    D. compression

71. Shear walls CANNOT be constructed using

I.   reinforced concrete
II. reinforced masonry
III. unreinforced masonry
IV. steel
V.   wood stud walls

    A. I only
    B. III only
    C. IV and V only
    D. II, III, and IV only

72. Which of the following statements about the concrete system known as the *hyperbolic paraboloid* is true?

    A. It acts as a beam in the long direction and as an arch in the short direction.
    B. It is a barrel shell with a single wide span.
    C. It consists of folded concrete plates.
    D. It is a concrete shell with a double curvature.

73. Which of the following statements about precast concrete is FALSE?

    A. It offers the advantage of fast construction.

    B. It is always prestressed and is therefore used for long spans.

    C. It is often produced under controlled factory conditions.

    D. It has a high heat insulation value.

74. A two-story residential building is being planned for a site in Washington state. The values of the mapped spectral response accelerations at a period of 0.2 sec and 1.0 sec, respectively, are 0.5 and 0.15. The structure is to have a total height of 24 ft (7.3 m). Soil reports suggest a soil profile that is mainly rock (site class B). A bearing wall system with reinforced concrete walls is proposed (R is 4).

Use Tables 8 and 9, Values of Site Coefficients F_a and F_v, in the Appendix. The upper limit value of the seismic response coefficient is 0.068. The lower limit is 0.01. Using the IBC and the lateral equivalent force procedure, what is the approximate base shear value as a percentage of the effective seismic building weight?

    A. 3% of the building's weight

    B. 5% of the building's weight

    C. 7% of the building's weight

    D. 10% of the building's weight

75. According to the ACI code requirements, what is the maximum permissible spacing of lateral ties in a reinforced concrete column?

    A. 16 times the diameter of the reinforcing bars

    B. 48 times the diameter of the lateral ties

    C. the least dimension of the column

    D. the least of the three dimensions listed above

76. Torsional effects

I. are significant in buildings of asymmetrical shapes such as buildings with L-configurations

II. are significant in buildings of symmetrical shapes and symmetrical shear-resisting elements

III. can be reduced by locating the shear-resisting elements around the perimeter of the building

IV. can be reduced by creating symmetry in the building and its shear-resisting elements

    A. II only

    B. I and IV only

    C. II and III only

    D. I, III, and IV only

77. A flat reinforced concrete slab is supported on columns only. The column grid is 24 ft by 24 ft (7.3 m by 7.3 m). The tributary area of a typical interior column is most nearly

    A. 140 ft² (13 m²)

    B. 290 ft² (27 m²)

    C. 390 ft² (36 m²)

    D. 580 ft² (53 m²)

78. The IBC requires that a certain amount of accidental torsion be considered even when a building is symmetrical. Why? (Choose the four that apply.)

    A. to allow for nonuniform vertical loading

    B. to allow for asymmetrical floor openings

    C. to reduce the effect of overturning moments

    D. to reduce drift

    E. to allow for eccentricity in rigidity due to non-structural elements and seismic ground motion

    F. to allow for the fact that positions of loads in an occupied building cannot be exactly determined

79. The overall thickness of a one-way reinforced concrete slab is often determined based on the ACI code provisions for minimum thickness. According to these provisions, what should be the overall thickness for a cantilevered concrete slab if the slab span is 11 ft (3.4 m)?

    A. 5.0 in (120 mm)

    B. 5.5 in (140 mm)

    C. 7.0 in (170 mm)

    D. 13 in (340 mm)

80. A reinforced concrete beam with a rectangular cross section has a width of 15 in (380) and an effective depth of 22 in (560). The reinforcement ratio is 0.0142. The minimum required reinforcing steel area for this beam is most nearly

    A. 2.4 in² (1500 mm²)
    B. 4.7 in² (3000 mm²)
    C. 5.3 in² (3400 mm²)
    D. 9.4 in² (6100 mm²)

81. Which of the following factors affect a building's response to an earthquake? (Choose the four that apply.)

    A. soil type
    B. local temperature
    C. building form
    D. building orientation
    E. building weight
    F. structural materials and system

82. What is the most common stud spacing in wood stud walls of conventional construction?

    A. 12 in (300)
    B. 16 in (400)
    C. 18 in (460)
    D. 24 in (600)

83. What is the shape of the steel studs used in a steel stud wall?

    A. channel
    B. I-section
    C. T-section
    D. tubes

84. The IBC requires that all buildings in seismic design categories D, E, and F be provided with accelerographs if

I. located within five miles of a known fault
II. built before 1975
III. more than six stories tall and having an aggregate floor area of at least 60,000 ft² (5574 m²)
IV. more than ten stories tall

    A. either I or II
    B. either I or IV
    C. either II or III
    D. either III or IV

85. Masonry is

    A. strong in tension and weak in compression
    B. strong in compression and weak in tension
    C. strong in both tension and compression
    D. weak in both tension and compression

86. A flexible diaphragm has a maximum lateral deformation of at least

    A. the average story drift of the story it's designed for
    B. two times the average story drift of the story it's designed for
    C. three times the average story drift of the story it's designed for
    D. four times the average story drift of the story it's designed for

87. Which of the following statements about tilt-up walls is FALSE?

    A. Tilt-up walls are reinforced concrete walls that are precast generally in a flat position and later tilted up to a vertical position.
    B. Tilt-up walls are subject to high stresses during construction.
    C. Exterior columns used with tilt-up walls must be precast concrete columns.
    D. Tilt-up walls provide a good fire resistance, great strength, and low maintenance.

88. Which two of these statements are correct?

I. In a flexible diaphragm, lateral loads are transferred to the vertical resisting elements according to tributary area.
II. In a rigid diaphragm, the lateral loads are transferred to the vertical resisting elements in proportion to the relative stiffness of these elements.
III. In a flexible diaphragm, the lateral loads are transferred to the vertical resisting elements in proportion to the relative stiffness of these elements.
IV. In a rigid diaphragm, the lateral loads are transferred to the vertical resisting elements according to tributary area.

    A. I and II
    B. I and IV
    C. II and III
    D. III and IV

89. A mat foundation is

A. one large footing that covers the entire floor area

B. one footing used for two columns when the two columns are close

C. a certain type of pile

D. a reinforced concrete slab placed on top of piles to help distribute the loads to the piles

90. Which of the following floor plans represents the best design for lateral loads?

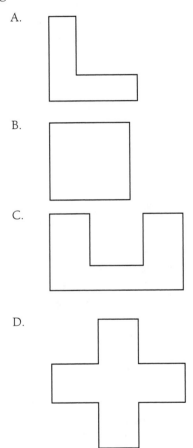

91. A raft, or compensated, footing is a

A. shallow mat foundation

B. mat foundation placed deep in the soil

C. certain type of pile

D. type of retaining wall

92. A soil's load-bearing capacity

A. increases with depth

B. decreases with depth

C. is not related to the depth

D. is related only to the soil type

93. Which of the following building elevations is problematic for lateral loads and must be avoided?

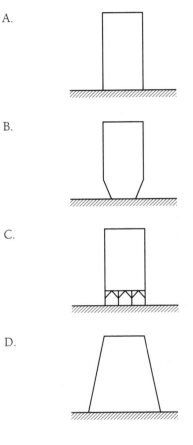

94. Which of the following types of piles has the lowest initial cost and least load-bearing capacity?

A. steel piles

B. precast concrete piles

C. cast-in-place concrete piles

D. timber piles

95. Which of the following statements about reentrant corners is FALSE?

    A. Reentrant corners are not allowed by building codes and must be avoided.

    B. If a reentrant corner cannot be avoided, then drag struts can be used to help transfer lateral loads properly.

    C. If a reentrant corner cannot be avoided, then a seismic separation could be provided.

    D. If a reentrant corner cannot be avoided, then providing a seismic separation is preferred as opposed to drag struts.

96. For earth of a depth between 10 ft and 20 ft (3 m and 6 m), the most efficient type of retaining wall is

    A. a gravity wall

    B. a cantilever wall

    C. a counterfort wall

    D. either a gravity or a counterfort wall

97. Adding a shear key to the base of a cantilever retaining wall helps prevent

    A. sliding of the wall

    B. overturning of the wall

    C. breaking and cracking of the wall base

    D. simultaneous breaking and overturning of the wall

98. Which of the following statements about base isolation is FALSE?

    A. Base isolation consists of isolating the building from the ground using steel and rubber bearings and dampers.

    B. The use of base isolation is likely to increase in the future.

    C. Base isolation is used in new buildings only, and cannot be applied to existing structures.

    D. Base isolation is used as an earthquake design solution.

99. According to the IBC, a soft story is a story in which

    A. the lateral stiffness is less than 70% of that in the story above or less than 80% of the average stiffness of the stories above

    B. the lateral stiffness is less than 60% of that in the story above or less than 70% of the average stiffness of the stories above

    C. the lateral stiffness is less than 50% of that in the story above or less than 60% of the average stiffness of the stories above

    D. the story lateral strength is less than 80% of that of the story above

100. Prior to designing and building the Eiffel Tower in Paris, the French engineer Gustave Eiffel was mainly known for designing and building

    A. concrete bridges

    B. iron bridges

    C. dams

    D. department stores

101. The Italian contractor and engineer Pier Luigi Nervi is most known for designing and building

    A. concrete domes and shell roofs

    B. timber homes

    C. steel skyscrapers

    D. concrete bridges

102. Which of the following earthquake effects or damages are NOT covered by the building codes?

I. ground shaking
II. landslides
III. soil liquefaction
IV. avalanches

    A. IV only

    B. II and III

    C. II, III, and IV

    D. I, II, III, and IV

103. The most flexible, or least rigid, lateral load resisting system uses

    A. shear walls
    B. concentric braced frames
    C. eccentric braced frames
    D. moment-resisting frames

104. What is the name of the structural engineer who designed both the Sears Tower and the John Hancock Building in Chicago?

    A. Felix Candela
    B. Leslie Robertson
    C. Fazlur Kahn
    D. Othmar Ammann

105. The moment-resisting frames known in the IBC as "intermediate moment-resisting frames" CANNOT generally be used in which of the following seismic design categories?

    A. category F only
    B. categories A and B
    C. categories D and E
    D. categories E and F

106. William Le Baron Jenney is an architect and engineer who is most known for designing the first steel-framed building in the United States, the

    A. Reliance Building in Chicago
    B. Fuller Building in New York City
    C. Woolworth Building in New York City
    D. Home Life Insurance Building in Chicago

107 In the lateral load resisting system known in the IBC as the dual system, the moment-resisting frame must be capable of resisting

    A. at least 25% of the base shear
    B. at least 50% of the base shear
    C. at least 80% of the base shear
    D. 100% of the base shear

108. The Yale University Skating Rink designed by Eero Saarinen is an example of a

    A. cable roof structure
    B. concrete shell structure
    C. tensioned fabric roof structure
    D. regular steel structure

109. What is the approximate thickness of the concrete walls supporting Rome's Pantheon dome?

    A. 20 in
    B. 2.0 ft
    C. 20 ft
    D. 40 ft

110. According to the IBC, a plan structural irregularity can be due to openings in the diaphragm system when the total open area exceeds _____% of the gross enclosed diaphragm area? (Fill in the blank.)

111. What were the main materials used in building the Crystal Palace in London?

    A. glass and reinforced concrete
    B. steel and aluminum
    C. timber and aluminum
    D. glass, cast iron, and wrought iron

112. According to the IBC, what is the period of vibration of a building if its approximate period of vibration, T_a, is 0.40 sec and the design spectral response acceleration parameter at 1 sec is 0.15? Use Table 5, Coefficient for Upper Limit on Calculated Period, in the Appendix.

    A. 0.25 sec
    B. 0.40 sec
    C. 0.64 sec
    D. 1.0 sec

113. What engineer or firm designed the glass tent of the Munich Olympic Stadium in Germany?

    A. Frei Otto
    B. Leslie Robertson
    C. Weidlinger Associates
    D. Ove Arup & Partners

114. To minimize the risk of pounding, a seismic separation must be provided between two adjacent buildings. This seismic separation should be equal to

    A. 5% of the taller building's height

    B. 10% of the shorter building's height, modified by a safety factor

    C. the sum of the expected drifts of the two buildings

    D. the sum of the expected drifts of the two buildings, modified by a safety factor

115. In cast-in-place concrete construction, the cost of the formwork roughly represents what percentage of total construction costs?

    A. less than 10%

    B. about 25%

    C. about 33%

    D. more than 50%

116. A building in an earthquake-prone area is designed to have an open front and shear walls around the other three sides. This constitutes an irregularity. What is the correct and most practical solution in this case?

    A. add drag struts to the front

    B. provide a moment-resisting frame in the front

    C. increase the safety factors in the design calculations

    D. change the entire design and close the front with a shear wall

117. A two-story residential building has a total height of 24 ft (7.3 m). The building has a bearing wall system with reinforced concrete walls. Use Table 6, Values of Approximate Period Parameters C_t and x, in the Appendix. According to the IBC and ASCE/SEI 7, the approximate period of vibration is

    A. 0.22 sec

    B. 0.28 sec

    C. 0.35 sec

    D. 0.48 sec

118. In a typical building, such as a conventional office building, the cost of the structure is generally what percentage of the total cost of construction?

    A. from 10% to 20%

    B. from 25% to 30%

    C. from 50% to 60%

    D. more than 75%

119. Which one of the following steel types is NOT normally used in the manufacture of bolts for structural steel connections?

    A. A36

    B. A325

    C. A490

    D. A449

120. The design moment due to a seismic load of 48 psf (2.3 kPa) on a concrete parapet wall that is 4 ft (1.2 m) high is approximately

    A. 190 ft-lbf per foot of parapet width (850 N·m per meter of parapet width)

    B. 380 ft-lbf per foot of parapet width (1700 N·m per meter of parapet width)

    C. 770 ft-lbf per foot of parapet width (3500 N·m per meter of parapet width)

    D. 1500 ft-lbf per foot of parapet width (6700 N·m per meter of parapet width)

121. Two ³/₈ in plates are connected to a ¹/₂ in plate using three bolts with a nominal diameter of ⁷/₈ in. The bolts are standard round bolts made of A325. The connection is of the bearing type, with threads included in the shear plane. The plates are made of A36 steel with a minimum tensile strength of 58 ksi. Use Table 2, Shear Bolt Values, and Table 14, Bearing Bolt Values, in the Appendix. What approximately is the maximum allowable load for this connection?

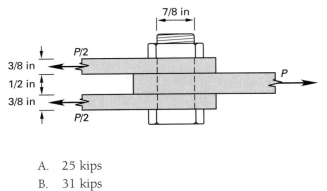

A.   25 kips
B.   31 kips
C.   76 kips
D.   92 kips

122. What is the average number of tornadoes reported in the United States each year?

A.   fewer than 100
B.   approximately 300
C.   500 to 600
D.   approximately 1000

123. A truss is loaded as shown. In kips (kilonewtons), the force in the member EF is ____. (Fill in the blank.)

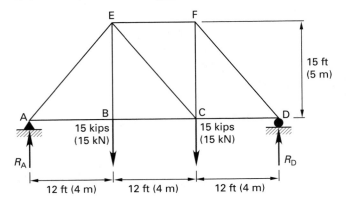

124. What was the magnitude of the 1906 San Francisco earthquake on the Richter scale?

A.   5.9
B.   6.5
C.   8.3
D.   9.2

125. According to the IBC, in which seismic design categories can the equivalent lateral force method always be used?

A.   categories A and B only
B.   categories A, B, and C only
C.   categories A, B, C, and D only
D.   categories A, B, C, D, E, and F

PRACTICE EXAM: VIGNETTE

STRUCTURAL LAYOUT VIGNETTE

Directions

Create a two-level roof framing solution based on the given floor plan and program requirements. The layout you design should be structurally sound and efficient.

Your layout should show the location of columns and/or load-bearing walls, the placement of beams, and the placement and spacing of roof joists. You may not add walls. All walls are assumed to be non-load-bearing unless you designate them otherwise. Indicate the span direction of decking. (On the actual exam, the software will include tools to designate load-bearing walls and indicate span direction.)

Program

The building is a small sewing shop used by well-known designers of women's clothing to inspect and repair garments before they are shipped to stores in different areas. The preliminary floor plan of this shop is given, and you are required to develop a roof framing layout for the building. The layout must accommodate the conditions and requirements given below.

Site and Foundation

1. The site has no seismic or wind pressure requirements.

2. The soils and foundation system are adequate for normal loads.

3. Concentrated and special loads need not be considered.

Construction and Materials

1. A steel structural system consisting of open web joists has been chosen for the roof structure.

2. Steel beam sections are to be rolled.

3. The metal deck on the joists is capable of carrying design loads on spans up to and including 5 ft (1525).

4. Joists are sized to carry roof loads only.

General Requirements

1. All roof framing is flat.

2. Cantilevers should not be used.

3. Columns may be located within walls, including the window wall and the clerestory window wall.

4. Any wall shown on the floor plan may be designated as a bearing wall. Additional bearing walls are not allowed.

5. Lintels must be shown at all openings in bearing walls.

6. The shop sewing area must be free of columns.

7. The corridor area must be free of columns.

8. Window walls extend to the underside of the structure above.

9. The roof over the shop's sewing area must be higher than the roof over the other areas. The roof over the sewing area is 16 ft (4880) above the floor. The roof over the other areas is 12 ft (3660) above the floor.

10. The structure must accommodate a clerestory window to be located along the full length of the sewing area's south wall.

Tips

- On the actual exam, draw the structural elements for the lower roof framing first. Then switch layers and draw the additional structural elements required for the upper roof framing. To be scored, the solution must be drawn on the two separate layers.

- To select an element overlapped by other elements, keep clicking without moving the mouse until the desired element is highlighted.

Warnings

- On the actual exam, the *draw joists* tool works like a two-point rectangle and allows the direction and spacing of joists to be selected. Do not draw individual joists.

- On the actual exam, the *draw decking* tool also works like a two-point rectangle and allows the direction of the joists to be selected.

Tools

Useful tools include the following.

- *zoom* tool for checking the location of elements
- full-screen cursor to help line up structural elements

Target Time: 1 hour

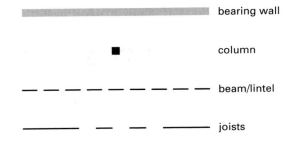

bearing wall

column

beam/lintel

joists

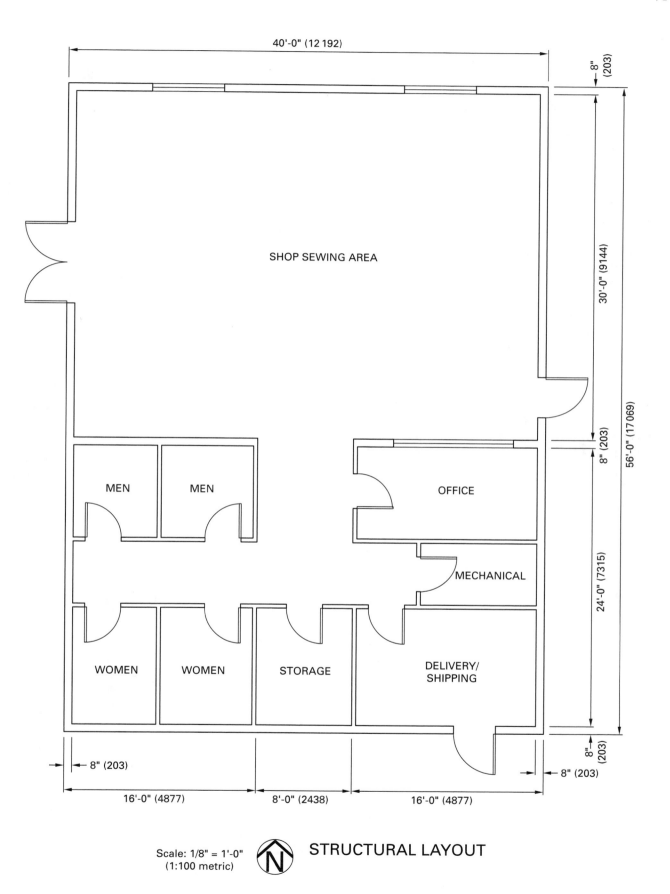

40'-0" (12 192)

8" (203)

30'-0" (9144)

56'-0" (17069)

SHOP SEWING AREA

8" (203)

24'-0" (7315)

MEN   MEN

OFFICE

MECHANICAL

WOMEN   WOMEN   STORAGE

DELIVERY/
SHIPPING

8" (203)

8" (203)

8" (203)

16'-0" (4877)   8'-0" (2438)   16'-0" (4877)

Scale: 1/8" = 1'-0"
(1:100 metric)

STRUCTURAL LAYOUT

PRACTICE EXAM: MULTIPLE CHOICE SOLUTIONS

1. B
2. A
3. C
4. D
5. A
6. B
7. C
8. A
9. A
10. C
11. A
12. A B D F
13. D
14. B
15. B
16. A
17. A
18. A B E F
19. D E
20. D
21. D
22. B C D
23. C
24. A D E
25. B

26. A
27. B
28. C
29. B
30. D
31. C
32. C
33. A
34. A
35. _____ **43** _____
36. B
37. B
38. _____ **8** _____
39. A
40. C
41. C
42. D
43. D
44. B
45. D
46. C
47. D
48. B
49. A
50. D

51. C
52. B
53. A
54. A
55. B
56. B
57. C
58. C
59. D
60. B
61. A
62. A
63. B
64. D
65. C
66. A
67. D
68. D
69. B
70. A
71. B
72. D
73. B
74. C
75. D

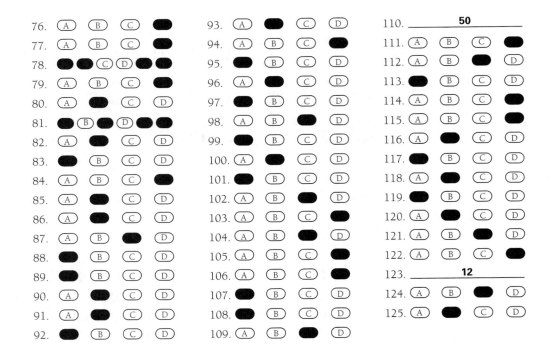

76. Ⓐ Ⓑ Ⓒ ●
77. Ⓐ Ⓑ Ⓒ ●
78. ● ● Ⓒ Ⓓ ● ●
79. Ⓐ Ⓑ Ⓒ ●
80. Ⓐ ● Ⓒ Ⓓ
81. ● Ⓑ ● Ⓓ ● ●
82. Ⓐ ● Ⓒ Ⓓ
83. ● Ⓑ Ⓒ Ⓓ
84. Ⓐ Ⓑ Ⓒ ●
85. Ⓐ ● Ⓒ Ⓓ
86. Ⓐ ● Ⓒ Ⓓ
87. Ⓐ Ⓑ ● Ⓓ
88. ● Ⓑ Ⓒ Ⓓ
89. ● Ⓑ Ⓒ Ⓓ
90. Ⓐ ● Ⓒ Ⓓ
91. Ⓐ ● Ⓒ Ⓓ
92. ● Ⓑ Ⓒ Ⓓ

93. Ⓐ ● Ⓒ Ⓓ
94. Ⓐ Ⓑ Ⓒ ●
95. ● Ⓑ Ⓒ Ⓓ
96. Ⓐ ● Ⓒ Ⓓ
97. ● Ⓑ Ⓒ Ⓓ
98. Ⓐ Ⓑ ● Ⓓ
99. ● Ⓑ Ⓒ Ⓓ
100. Ⓐ ● Ⓒ Ⓓ
101. ● Ⓑ Ⓒ Ⓓ
102. Ⓐ Ⓑ ● Ⓓ
103. Ⓐ Ⓑ Ⓒ ●
104. Ⓐ Ⓑ ● Ⓓ
105. Ⓐ Ⓑ Ⓒ ●
106. Ⓐ Ⓑ Ⓒ ●
107. ● Ⓑ Ⓒ Ⓓ
108. ● Ⓑ Ⓒ Ⓓ
109. Ⓐ Ⓑ ● Ⓓ

110. _____ **50** _____
111. Ⓐ Ⓑ Ⓒ ●
112. Ⓐ Ⓑ ● Ⓓ
113. ● Ⓑ Ⓒ Ⓓ
114. Ⓐ Ⓑ Ⓒ ●
115. Ⓐ Ⓑ Ⓒ ●
116. Ⓐ ● Ⓒ Ⓓ
117. ● Ⓑ Ⓒ Ⓓ
118. Ⓐ ● Ⓒ Ⓓ
119. ● Ⓑ Ⓒ Ⓓ
120. Ⓐ ● Ⓒ Ⓓ
121. Ⓐ Ⓑ ● Ⓓ
122. Ⓐ Ⓑ Ⓒ ●
123. _____ **12** _____
124. Ⓐ Ⓑ ● Ⓓ
125. Ⓐ ● Ⓒ Ⓓ

1. The answer is B.

The primary force and its components form a triangle as shown in the problem illustration. Two of the angles are given as 40° and 80°, so the third angle is 180° − (40° + 80°) = 60°.

Apply the law of sines to the triangle of forces.

$$\frac{a}{\sin A} = \frac{b}{\sin B} = \frac{c}{\sin C}$$

$$\frac{100}{\sin 60°} = \frac{F_1}{\sin 80°} = \frac{F_2}{\sin 40°}$$

Solve for F_1 and F_2.

$$F_1 = \frac{(100)\sin 80°}{\sin 60°} = 113.72 \quad (110)$$

$$F_2 = \frac{(100)\sin 40°}{\sin 60°} = 74.22 \quad (74)$$

2. The answer is A.

Compared to hurricanes, tornadoes generally are smaller in diameter and have faster wind speeds.

A tornado consists of a funnel-shaped rotating column of air that emerges from a cumuliform cloud. The average base diameter is 500 ft (150 m) across. While tornado wind speeds average 250 mph (400 km/h), they can exceed 500 mph (800 km/h).

A hurricane also consists of a rotating column of air, but it must form over water. Hurricanes may be 10 mi to 50 mi (16 km to 80 km) wide. Wind speeds must be in excess of 74 mph (34 m/s) to be classified as a hurricane. Sustained winds of more than 190 mph (85 m/s) have been measured.

3. The answer is C.

Write the static equations of equilibrium.

In U.S. units:

The sum of the moments about point A is zero.

$$\Sigma M_A = 0$$
$$Px_1 - R_BL = 0$$
$$-(7000 \text{ lbf})(8 \text{ ft}) + R_B(12 \text{ ft}) = 0$$
$$R_B = 4666.67 \text{ lbf} \quad (4700 \text{ lbf})$$

The sum of the forces is zero.

$$\Sigma F_y = 0$$
$$R_A + R_B - P = 0$$
$$R_A + 4666.67 \text{ lbf} - 7000 \text{ lbf} = 0$$
$$R_A = 2333.33 \text{ lbf} \quad (2300 \text{ lbf})$$

In SI units:

The sum of the moments about point A is zero.

$$\Sigma M_A = 0$$
$$Px_1 - R_BL = 0$$
$$-(4000 \text{ N})(3 \text{ m}) + R_B(4 \text{ m}) = 0$$
$$R_B = 3000 \text{ N}$$

The sum of the forces is zero.

$$\Sigma F_y = 0$$
$$R_A + R_B - P = 0$$
$$R_A + 3000 \text{ N} - 4000 \text{ N} = 0$$
$$R_A = 1000 \text{ N}$$

4. The answer is D.

Wind speed varies with height. So that wind measurements carried out at different wind stations can be compared, all wind is measured a standard height of 33 ft (10 m) above the ground surface.

5. The answer is A.

Stress in a body is the internal resistance to deformation or to the action of the external force.

6. The answer is B.

The windward wall gets direct (positive) pressure, and the leeward wall gets suction (negative) pressure.

7. The answer is C.

The stress, f, is obtained by dividing the force, F, by the cross-sectional area, A, of the rod.

In U.S. units:

The cross-sectional area is

$$A = \pi r^2 = \pi(1 \text{ in})^2 = 3.14 \text{ in}^2$$

The tension stress in the rod is

$$f = \frac{F}{A} = \frac{10{,}000 \text{ lbf}}{3.14 \text{ in}^2} = 3185 \text{ psi} \quad (3200 \text{ psi})$$

In SI units:

The cross-sectional area is

$$A = \pi r^2 = \pi (25 \text{ mm}^2) = 1960 \text{ mm}^2$$

The tension stress in the rod is

$$f = \frac{F}{A} = \frac{5000 \text{ N}}{1960 \text{ mm}^2} = 2.6 \text{ N/mm}^2 \quad (2.6 \text{ MPa})$$

8. **The answer is A.**

Corners and eaves generally receive higher wind forces than the rest of a building. This is why most wind damage occurs at corners and eaves.

9. **The answer is A.**

The gap should be 0.079 in (1.5).

The total elongation due to the rise in temperature is

$$\delta = \alpha L \Delta t$$

α is the coefficient of linear expansion, L is the original length in inches (millimeters), and Δt is the change in temperature.

Since all slabs are similar and have the same length, the gap between the slabs should equal the total elongation of a slab.

In U.S. units:

The total elongation due to the rise in temperature is

$$\delta = \left(5.5 \times 10^{-6} \frac{\text{in}}{\text{in·°F}} \right)(480 \text{ in})(85°F - 55°F)$$

$$= 0.079 \text{ in}$$

In SI units:

The total elongation due to the rise in temperature is

$$\delta = \left(9.9 \times 10^{-6} \frac{\text{mm}}{\text{mm·°C}} \right)(10\,000 \text{ mm})(30°C - 15°C)$$

$$= 1.5 \text{ mm}$$

10. **The answer is C.**

The direct wind pressure on a vertical surface is directly proportional to the square of the wind velocity. This pressure, p, also called "stagnation pressure," is related to the basic wind velocity, v, by the following formula.

In U.S. units:

$$p_{psf} = 0.00256 v_{mph}^2$$

In this formula, the wind pressure is measured in pounds-force per square foot, and the basic wind velocity is measured in miles per hour.

In SI units:

$$p_{N/m^2} = 0.613 v_{m/s}^2$$

The wind pressure in this formula is measured in newtons per square meter, and the wind velocity is measured in meters per second.

11. **The answer is A.**

Sign conventions identify both the bending moment that creates compression stresses in the top fibers of a beam and tension stresses in the bottom fibers of a beam as a positive bending moment. The tension and compression stresses are reversed in choice B, so B is incorrect.

12. **The answer is A, B, D, and F.**

Wind pressure on a building is affected by wind speed, surrounding terrain, and the building's height and shape. The weight of the building and the soil type do not affect it.

13. **The answer is D.**

The moment of inertia of a rectangle about its horizontal centroidal axis (I_x) is

$$I_x = \frac{bd^3}{12}$$

In this equation, b is the width of the section and d is its depth.

In U.S. units:

$$I_x = \frac{(5 \text{ in})(8 \text{ in})^3}{12} = 213 \text{ in}^4 \quad (210 \text{ in}^4)$$

In SI units:

$$I_x = \frac{(120 \text{ mm})(200 \text{ mm})^3}{12} = 0.80 \times 10^8 \text{ mm}^4$$

14. **The answer is B.**

In a simply supported beam, the largest shear force is always located at one of the two beam supports. The two beam support reactions become equal when loads are applied symmetrically.

15. **The answer is B.**

Because the effects of tornadoes are difficult to represent and consider, they are not covered in building codes or considered on the wind speed map. Wind velocity and direction change very quickly in a tornado, and wind researchers have difficulty modeling tornadoes in wind laboratories. The basic rules of design for high winds are generally applied for tornado-prone regions. Tornado shelters are most often designed for a wind velocity of 300 mph.

16. **The answer is A.**

The most widely used structural steel in buildings is ASTM A36. This steel is weldable and belongs to the category of carbon steels. A242 and A588 steels are from the category of corrosion-resistant, high-strength, low-alloy steels. They are often used in outdoor structures and bridges. A514 steel belongs to the category of quenched and tempered alloy. It is a very high-strength steel that is generally available in plates and bars but not in rolled beam shapes.

17. **The answer is A.**

A building's lateral (side-to-side) displacement due to wind forces is called *drift*.

18. **The answer is A, B, E, and F.**

Excessive beam deflection is visually disturbing and might give the impression that the beam is not safe when it is. An excessive deflection could also damage adjacent building materials, breaking windows or cracking partitions and suspended plaster ceilings.

A beam can have a large deflection and still be safe in bending and shear. Therefore choices C and D are incorrect.

The deflection limits recommended by building codes and standards are often calculated as a percentage of the span. For instance, a limitation of 1/240 or 1/300 of the span length, calculated under the total load applied on the beam including all dead and live loads, is often recommended for steel beams so that their appearance is not disturbing. For beams and girders supporting plastered ceilings, a limitation of 1/360 of the span length, calculated under live load only, is often recommended. This last limitation is explicit

in the AISC Specification, and is frequently used as a guide whether plaster ceilings are used or not.

19. **The answer is D and E.**

It is necessary to limit drift (side-to-side motion) because it can cause discomfort to the occupants of a building, especially near the top of the structure. Drift can also cause damage to brittle elements in the buildings. Base shear is associated with earthquakes, not wind force, so choice A is incorrect. Drift is not the main cause of torsion, so choice B is incorrect. Drift is not limited because of its appearance, and does not create an overturning moment, so choices C and F are incorrect. The overturning moment is created by the lateral forces, not drift.

20. **The answer is D.**

The equation used to calculate the deflection of a steel beam is

$$\Delta = \frac{KPL^3}{EI}$$

K is a constant that depends on the type of load applied on the beam, P is the load on the beam, L is the length of the span, E is the modulus of elasticity (which is a constant for all steel types), and I is the moment of inertia of the section. The beam deflection varies directly with the load applied on the beam and the length of the span cubed. It is inversely proportional to the moment of inertia of the section. Statements I, II, and IV are correct.

The yield stress of the steel, F_y, does not appear in the equation and has no effect on the deflection value. Therefore, statement III is incorrect.

21. **The answer is D.**

On the map of basic wind speeds, special wind regions are areas that are excluded from the map and for which wind speeds must be determined from local records. These regions have a topography and conditions that are quite variable, and they are often very different from their surrounding areas. These regions include the Pacific Northwest coast, the shores of the Great Lakes, and the mountains and canyons of Southern California.

22. **The answer is B, C, and D.**

In the lateral buckling of steel beams with I-sections, it is the compression flange that buckles. In the most common beam type, the simply supported beam, the compression flange is the top flange, so in order to prevent the lateral buckling of the beam it is necessary to prevent the top compression flange from buckling. This can be achieved by encasing the top flange in concrete or by welding the metal decking to it. Lateral buckling can also be prevented by encasing the entire beam in concrete.

Encasing the tension flange (bottom flange) in concrete will not prevent the lateral buckling of the top flange, so choice A is incorrect. Lateral buckling cannot be totally prevented based on shape selection, so choice E is incorrect. Providing intermediate lateral support in the form of bracing at any spacing will only reduce the lateral buckling, and might not be sufficient to totally prevent it; so choice F is incorrect.

23.   The answer is C.

The gradient height is 1500 ft (460 m) for urban or metropolitan areas. Choice A, 900 ft (270 m), is the gradient height in an open country area. Choice B, 1200 ft (370 m), is the gradient height for suburban areas. Choice D, 2000 ft (610 m), does not apply to any established area.

24.   The answer is A, D, and E.

In the ASCE/SEI 7 wind design method, factor K_z (velocity pressure exposure coefficient evaluated at height z) takes into account building height, exposure, and wind gusting. The occupancy type (choice F) is considered by means of a separate factor called the *importance factor*. The building's orientation and weight are not related to this factor, and are not considered in wind design

25.   The answer is B.

The tendency of a column to buckle increases with the slenderness ratio KL/r, where K is the effective length factor, L is the column length, and r is the radius of gyration.

From the equation, it is clear that the slenderness ratio increases with an increase in the length and a decrease in the radius of gyration. The answer is, therefore, choice B.

26.   The answer is A.

The risk of overturning is higher in buildings with a high height-to-width ratio. Top-heavy buildings generally overturn more easily than bottom- or base-heavy buildings.

27.   The answer is B.

The support reactions of this beam are equal, and each reaction is equal to one-half the total load applied on the beam. This is because the loads are applied in a symmetrical manner on the beam; therefore, each reaction is 7 kips (7 kN). The shear diagram should start with the value of the reaction, 7 kips (7 kN), on the left and should remain constant over the first 3 ft (3 m), meaning that it should remain horizontal for that distance. The diagram should then drop vertically at 3 ft (3 m) for the amount of the load applied there, 7 kips (7 kN), which will bring the shear value down to zero. The shear remains zero over the next 4 ft (4 m) and then drops again vertically downward for the amount of the second point load of 7 kips (7 kN). This brings the shear value down to −7 kips (−7 kN). It remains −7 kips (−7 kN) for the last 3 ft (3 m), then the diagram goes vertically upward at the right support for the amount of the support reaction there, 7 kips (7 kN), which completes the shear diagram. The correct diagram is B.

In choices A and D, the shear is not equal to zero between the point loads. Choice C shows the bending moment diagram for this beam.

28.   The answer is C.

The most economical safe size for this beam is selected based on the value of the minimum required section modulus (S_{req}), using Table 11, Allowable Stress Design Selection.

The minimum required section modulus is calculated by dividing the maximum bending moment, M_{max}, by the maximum allowable bending stress, F_b.

$$S_{req} = \frac{M_{max}}{F_b}$$

The maximum bending moment for a simply supported beam loaded with a uniformly distributed load is calculated from the uniformly distributed load, w, and the span length, L.

$$\begin{aligned}
M_{max} &= \frac{wL^2}{8} \\
&= \frac{\left(3000 \, \frac{\text{lbf}}{\text{ft}}\right)(20 \text{ ft})^2}{8} \\
&= (150{,}000 \text{ ft-lbf})\left(12 \, \frac{\text{in}}{\text{ft}}\right) \\
&= 1{,}800{,}000 \text{ in-lbf} \quad (1800 \text{ in-kips})
\end{aligned}$$

The maximum allowable bending stress is calculated from the yield stress of the steel, F_y. For A36 steel, the yield stress has the value of 36 ksi.

$$F_b = 0.66F_y$$

$$= (0.66)\left(36\,\frac{\text{kips}}{\text{in}}\right) = 24\text{ ksi}$$

The minimum required section modulus is

$$S_{req} = \frac{1800\text{ in-kips}}{24\,\dfrac{\text{kips}}{\text{in}^2}} = 75\text{ in}^3$$

From the table, look under S_x for a value close to the minimum required value (75 in³), then select the boldfaced section that is the most economical, safe dimension for this beam: W21 × 44.

29.   The answer is B.

The moment-resisting frame has rigid moment-resisting connections between beams and columns, and it is an appropriate system to use for resisting lateral forces, not just in low-rise buildings, but also in high-rise buildings with 30 stories or less. For taller buildings, other systems should be considered, or some additional type of bracing, such as X or chevron bracing, should be used.

30.   The answer is D.

The most commonly used shapes for columns are the W shapes (statement II). These shapes can also be reinforced with flange plates if necessary (IV). Structural tubing in the form of square, rectangular, or round pipes are also common (III). Structural tees are not used as column shapes, so statement I is incorrect.

31.   The answer is C.

In U.S. units:

The basic wind velocity pressure in pounds-force per square foot is

$$q = 0.00256K_zK_{zt}K_dv^2I$$

The K_z factor is taken from Table 12. K_z is 0.57 for exposure B (downtown of a city), with a height of 14 ft and case 2. This factor combines the effects of height, exposure, and wind gusting.

K_{zt} is 1 for a flat site (the topographic factor).

K_d is 0.85 for buildings (the directionality factor).

v is 85 mph, which is the basic wind speed taken from Fig. 2.1.

The I factor, or importance factor, is a function of the building's occupancy type. This small commercial building is considered a category II, and the I factor should be taken as 1.

$$q = (0.00256)(0.57)(1)(0.85)\left(85\,\frac{\text{mi}}{\text{hr}}\right)^2(1)$$

$$= 8.96\text{ lbf/ft}^2 \quad (9.0\text{ psf})$$

In SI units:

The basic wind velocity pressure in newtons per square meter is

$$q = 0.613K_zK_{zt}K_dv^2I$$

The K_z factor is taken from Table 12. K_z is 0.57 for exposure B (downtown of a city), with a height of 4.3 m and case 2. This factor combines the effects of height, exposure, and wind gusting.

K_{zt} is 1 for a flat site (the topographic factor).

K_d is 0.85 for buildings (the directionality factor).

v is 38 m/s, which is the basic wind speed taken from Fig. 1.

The I factor, or importance factor, is a function of the building's occupancy type. This small commercial building is considered a category II, and the I factor should be taken as 1.

$$q = (0.613)(0.57)(1)(0.85)\left(38\,\frac{\text{m}}{\text{s}}\right)^2(1)$$

$$= 428.87\text{ N/m}^2 \quad (430\text{ N/m}^2)$$

32.   The answer is C.

The bending moment diagram should have the shape of a sloped line for a concentrated load type. This means that diagrams in choices A and D are incorrect. The diagram in A is a horizontal line and corresponds to the general shape of the shear diagram for this beam. Choice D shows a curved line, which corresponds to the bending moment diagram of a uniformly distributed load. The diagrams in B and C show a sloped line; however, the bending moment at the free left end of the cantilever beam should be equal to zero because the point load is applied there and has no moment at this point. This is shown in diagram C.

33.   The answer is A.

To determine the basic wind speed for San Francisco, refer to Fig. 1, the basic wind speed map of ASCE/SEI 7. This value is 85 mph (38 m/s).

34.   The answer is A.

The overturning moment at the base of the frame is calculated at the pivot, which is the point at the frame's lower right corner in the illustration. The overturning moment is caused by the lateral forces. The dead loads help stabilize the frame.

The moment of a force, M, is equal to the force, F, multiplied by its arm, d.

$$M = Fd$$

The total overturning moment about point B caused by the three lateral wind forces is the sum of the moments of these three forces about the point.

The overturning moment is the sum of the individual moments of the three applied lateral forces.

In U.S. units:

$$M_{overturning} = \sum Fd$$

$$= (5 \text{ kips})(11 \text{ ft}) + (10 \text{ kips})(22 \text{ ft})$$

$$+ (15 \text{ kips})(33 \text{ ft})$$

$$= 770 \text{ ft-kips}$$

In SI units:

$$M_{overturning} = \sum Fd$$

$$= (5 \text{ kN})(4 \text{ m}) + (10 \text{ kN})(8 \text{ m})$$

$$+ (15 \text{ kN})(12 \text{ m})$$

$$= 280 \text{ kN·m}$$

35.   The answer is 43.

Refer to Table 13. Select the effective length $KL = 11$ ft in the left column and review the section values in that row. The section to select should be able to carry at least 200 kips, so look in the white table sections (36 ksi) for the size with the lightest load over 200 kips, which is a W14 × 43. With an effective length of 11 ft, this section can carry up to 207 kips safely. This is the lightest and most economical section. The beam weight of this section is 43 lbf/ft.

36.   The answer is B.

Glulam beams are generally used for long spans and heavy loads because the structural properties and capacity of glulam generally exceed those of sawn lumber. The sizes and length of sawn lumber beams are limited by the sizes of the trees used to produce lumber. Glulam is fabricated from thin lams of wood that are glued together to produce members of nearly any size or length.

37.   The answer is B.

The parapet given is similar to a vertical cantilever beam subjected to a uniformly distributed load, so the resultant of the uniform load must be calculated first. The design moment is then determined by calculating the moment of this resultant.

In U.S. units:

The resultant of this load per foot of parapet, R, is calculated by multiplying the uniform load per unit length times the length of the span. This is done for a parapet width of 1 ft.

$$R = Phw = \left(12 \frac{\text{lbf}}{\text{ft}^2}\right)(3 \text{ ft})(1 \text{ ft}) = 36 \text{ lbf}$$

This resultant is assumed to be acting at the center of the span. Therefore its arm, with respect to the base of the parapet, is one half of the span. The moment per foot of parapet is then calculated by multiplying the resultant times its arm length.

$$M = Rd = R\left(\frac{h}{2}\right)$$

$$= (36 \text{ lbf})\left(\frac{3 \text{ ft}}{2}\right)$$

$$= 54 \text{ ft-lbf}$$

In SI units:

The resultant of this load per meter of parapet, R, is first calculated by multiplying the uniform load per unit length times the length of the span. This is done for a parapet width of 1 m.

$$R = Phw = \left(600 \, \frac{\text{N}}{\text{m}^2}\right)(0.9 \text{ m})(1 \text{ m}) = 540 \text{ N}$$

This resultant is assumed to be acting at the center of the span, so its arm, with respect to the base of the parapet, is one half of the span. The moment per meter of parapet is then calculated by multiplying the resultant times its arm length.

$$M = Rd = R\left(\frac{h}{2}\right)$$

$$= (540 \text{ N})\left(\frac{0.9 \text{ m}}{2}\right)$$

$$= 243 \text{ N·m} \quad (240 \text{ N·m})$$

38. The answer is 8.

From Table 1, select the size based on the value of the minimum required section modulus for the beam. As the normal loads will be vertical and thus perpendicular to the x-x axis, the section modulus about x-x is used.

$$S_{\text{req}} = \frac{M_{\text{max}}}{F'_b}$$

S_{req} is the minimum required section modulus, M_{max} is the maximum bending moment, and F'_b is the modified or adjusted allowable bending moment.

The maximum bending moment for a simply supported beam loaded with a uniformly distributed load is calculated from the total uniform load on the beam per foot, w, and the span length, L.

$$M_{\text{max}} = \frac{wL^2}{8}$$

$$= \frac{\left(27 \, \frac{\text{lbf}}{\text{ft}} + 53 \, \frac{\text{lbf}}{\text{ft}}\right)(12 \text{ ft})^2\left(12 \, \frac{\text{in}}{\text{ft}}\right)}{8}$$

$$= 17{,}280 \text{ in-lbf}$$

The modified allowable bending stress is calculated by multiplying the reference value of the allowable bending stress, F_b, by some adjustment factors according to the NDS.

$$F'_b = F_b C_M C_D C_t C_F C_r$$

C_M is the wet service factor, which is equal to 1 for dry conditions. C_D is the load duration factor; for a floor live load, C_D is equal to 1. C_t is the temperature factor and is equal to 1 for normal temperature. C_F is the size factor, and C_r is the repetitive member factor.

A certain average value for the factor C_F should be assumed first and then adjusted based on the calculated size. One of the possible values given for C_F in the problem can be used first, and the result can be adjusted up or down as needed. Assume C_F to be 1.3.

The problem suggests what is known as a *repetitive member system*. In a repetitive member system, three or more parallel beams of dimension lumber are used. Beams are spaced at 24 in on center or less. Elements are also connected by a load-distributing element such as a subfloor. The problem clearly indicates a typical beam in a floor framing that consists of several beams. The spacing is given as 16 in on center, which is less than 24 in. A subfloor generally connects these beams, so the repetitive member factor applies. The C_r factor has the value of 1.15 and applies to the allowable bending stress.

$$F'_b = \left(1000 \, \frac{\text{lbf}}{\text{in}^2}\right)(1)(1)(1)(1.3)(1.15) = 1495 \text{ lbf/in}^2$$

$$S_{\text{req}} = \frac{M_{\text{max}}}{F'_b} = \frac{17{,}280 \text{ in-lbf}}{1495 \, \dfrac{\text{lbf}}{\text{in}^2}} = 11.56 \text{ in}^3$$

In Table 1, look in the section modulus column and select the smallest size that satisfies the minimum required value of 11.56 in³, using a nominal thickness of 2 in. This is a 2×8 beam, with a section modulus of 13.14 in³.

Check the size factor, C_F, for a 2×8. This factor has the value of 1.2 and not 1.3 as assumed. An adjustment is therefore necessary.

Recalculate the modified allowable bending stress and the minimum required section modulus based on the size factor of 1.2.

$$F'_b = \left(1000 \, \frac{\text{lbf}}{\text{in}^2}\right)(1)(1)(1)(1.3)(1.15) = 1380 \text{ lbf/in}^2$$

$$S_{\text{req}} = \frac{M_{\text{max}}}{F'_b} = \frac{17{,}280 \text{ in-lbf}}{1380 \, \dfrac{\text{lbf}}{\text{in}^2}} = 12.52 \text{ in}^3$$

Look again in Table 1.4, this time for the smallest size that satisfies the minimum required value of 12.52 in³. This again gives a 2×8 beam, so this is the correct answer.

39.   The answer is A.

One diagonal brace is normally designed to be stressed in tension, while the other is not stressed. This is done to minimize costs. Diagonal braces are not designed to work in compression. By designing diagonal members as tension members instead of compression members, their size and therefore their cost is minimized. X-bracing is a common type of lateral bracing for tall structures. Bracing is often placed at the center of the structural framing, such as around the building's central core. When a wind load hits a building from one side, one of the braces acts in tension and the other one is not stressed. When the wind direction is reversed, the brace that works in tension is reversed accordingly while the other is not stressed.

40.   The answer is C.

Wood I-joists are generally used for spans larger than 20 ft (6 m), up to about 45 ft (13.7 m) or a little more, depending on the manufacturer.

The size of lumber is limited by the size of the trees from which it is made. For this reason, regular sawn lumber joists are usually available for spans up to about 20 ft (6 m). In wood buildings, and for spans larger than 20 ft (6 m), sawn lumber joists cannot be used and other options must be considered, such as I-joists and other engineered wood products like LVL (laminated veneer lumber) and glulam (glued laminated timber).

Wood I-joists have an I-section, with flanges made of lumber and a web made of plywood or oriented strand board (OSB). They are generally spaced like sawn lumber beams, and often frame into an LVL or a glulam beam in the perpendicular direction. They are usually available for spans up to about 45 ft (13.7 m).

41.   The answer is C.

The John Hancock Tower in Chicago was designed using a trussed tube system. The building's frame consists of a tube with X-braces at the perimeter on all four sides. The X-braces, each covering 18 stories, provide stability against the strong winds that blow over Lake Michigan.

The tower, which is 1105 ft (337 m) tall and has 100 stories, is a monolithic tube tapering elegantly from base to top floor. This design advanced skyscraper construction by incorporating wind-bracing elements into the building's exterior frame. It was designed by the firm Skidmore, Owings & Merrill (SOM).

42.   The answer is D.

The main benefit of using platform framing is the ease of construction resulting from utilizing the platform in each story for wall and partition frame preassembly.

43.   The answer is D.

The design for the Sears Tower in Chicago uses the bundled tube concept. The bundled tube is one of the most efficient structural systems against winds. The tower is a collection of nine framed tubes banded together for maximum support. Each tube is 75 ft (23 m) square, with no interior columns. The structure's most striking feature is its series of setbacks. All nine tubes rise for the first 49 stories; then some stop, leaving seven tubes up to the 65th floor, five up to the 90th floor, and only two all the way to the top.

The Sears Tower was designed by the firm Skidmore, Owings & Merrill (SOM). It was built between 1971 and 1974 to a height of 1469 ft (448 m). It has 110 stories and remained the world's tallest building until 1996 when it lost the title to the Petronas Towers in Malaysia.

44.   The answer is B.

Open-web steel joists are generally used with uniformly distributed loads, and the longer the span and the lighter the load, the more economical this system is. Heavy concentrated loads should be avoided with this system or should be treated with special care.

45.   The answer is D.

The answer is Taipei 101 in Taiwan. The Taipei Financial Center, known as Taipei 101, is in an area prone to both earthquakes and typhoons. The building's design includes a vibration damper to restrict excessive swaying from high winds. This vibration damper consists of a suspended steel ball weighing 650 tons (590 metric tons) installed on the 92nd floor of the building and visible on the inside.

The Taipei Financial Center was built from 1999 to 2004 to a height of 1667 ft (508 m), making it the world's tallest building. It will be overtaken when the Burj Dubai is completed, which is scheduled to be in late 2008.

46. The answer is C.

In the open-web steel joists structural system, the deep-long span joists of the DLH-series have depths of up to 6.0 ft (1.8 m).

Choice A is the limit depth for the open-web joists of the K-series. Choice B is the limit depth for open-web joists of the LH-series.

47. The answer is D.

Roof trusses resting on masonry walls are generally designed with diagonal bracing that often consists of round rods placed in the plane of the top chord in alternate bays. In addition, the lower chord is frequently braced with one or two lines of continuous struts, depending on the span. These struts are often steel angles, channels, or light beams.

48. The answer is B.

In wind design, the maximum permissible drift of one story relative to an adjacent story is 0.0025 times the story height.

In U.S. units:

The story height is 12 ft, and the maximum permissible drift is

$$d = 0.0025h$$
$$= (0.0025)(12 \text{ ft})\left(12 \frac{\text{in}}{\text{ft}}\right)$$
$$= 0.36 \text{ in}$$

In SI units:

The story height is 3.7 m, and the maximum permissible drift is

$$d = 0.0025h$$
$$= (0.0025)(3.7 \text{ mm})\left(1000 \frac{\text{mm}}{\text{m}}\right)$$
$$= 9.25 \text{ mm} \quad (9.2 \text{ mm})$$

49. The answer is A.

The false statement is choice A. In a steel dome, the ring at the bottom functions in tension, not compression, and is often referred to as the *tension ring*. The dome tends to open up at the bottom and exert outward thrusts continuously around the perimeter. These thrusts are resisted by the tension ring. All other statements about steel domes are true.

50. The answer is D.

Horizontal diaphragms can be constructed using plywood, particleboard, concrete, steel decking, or a combination of these materials.

51. The answer is C.

The false statement is choice C. In designing cable roof systems, the forces that require special consideration are the wind forces, not the gravity loads. Wind forces can cause vibration in cable roof systems, which can lead to failure if excessive. All other statements about cable-supported roofs are true.

52. The answer is B.

Like stone, concrete is a construction material that behaves well under compression but can crack easily under a small amount of tension. The answer is therefore choice B, compression. *Bending stress* (choice D) is a general term used for stress generated by the bending action of a beam under loading. A bending stress can be either tension or compression.

53. The answer is A.

The materials that cannot function as a diaphragm are straight tongue-and-groove sheathing and light-gauge corrugated metal. Concrete and plywood are often used as diaphragm materials.

54. The answer is A.

Prestressed concrete is reinforced concrete in which some initial compression stresses are introduced prior to loading. Concrete has a low tensile strength. Prestressing increases a concrete element's capacity to resist the tension stresses generated by loads.

55. The answer is B.

The Saffir-Simpson scale classifies hurricanes by severity, using categories numbered from 1 to 5. For example, category 1, the least severe, is for tropical storms that have sustained winds of 74 mph to 95 mph (119 km/h to 153 km/h), producing a storm surge of about 4 ft to 5 ft (1.2 m to 1.5 m) above normal water level. Damage is primarily to shrubbery, trees, foliage, unanchored mobile homes, and poorly constructed signs, with no real damage to other structures. Also possible are inundation of low-lying coastal roads, minor pier damage, and small crafts torn from moorings in exposed anchorage.

At the other extreme, category 5 applies to maximum sustained winds of more than 155 mi/hr (249 km/h) and a potential storm surge of more than 18 ft (5.5 m) above normal. Damage can include shrubs and trees blown down, considerable damage to roofs of buildings, all signs down, very severe and extensive damage to windows and doors, complete failure of roofs on many residences and industrial buildings, extensive shattering of glass in windows and doors, some complete building failure, small buildings overturned or blown away, complete destruction of mobile homes, major damage to lower floors of all structures less than 15 ft (4.5 m) above sea level within 500 yards (455 m) of shore, and low-lying escape routes inland cut by rising water three to five hours before hurricane center arrives. Massive evacuation may be required of residential areas on low ground within 5 mi to 10 mi (8 km to 16 km) of shore.

56.   The answer is B.

The two scales used to classify earthquakes are the Richter scale and the modified Mercalli scale.

The Richter scale was named after the American seismologist Charles Francis Richter (1900–1985). It classifies the energy released at the focus of an earthquake as measured by a seismometer or seismograph. The Richter scale classifies the magnitude of the earthquake. It is a logarithmic scale that uses numbers to indicate the earthquake's magnitude. The numbers range from 1 to 9, though in theory no upper limit exists.

The modified Mercalli scale classifies the effects of an earthquake on people and buildings. It was first introduced in the late 1800s by the Italian seismologist Giuseppe Mercalli (1850–1914), and it uses Roman numerals from I to XII.

Although there is no formal correlation between the two scales, intensities II to III on the Mercalli scale are roughly equal to magnitudes 3 to 4 on the Richter scale, and XI to XII to 8 to 9.

57.   The answer is C.

A flat plate is a simple, smooth concrete slab supported on columns only (choice C). A slab supported by beams on all four sides is known as a flat slab with beams. A system of beams and girders is used in a one-way slab system. Ribs are used in a waffle slab or pan joist system.

58.   The answer is C.

The location deep within the earth where the seismic movement of rock begins is called the *hypocenter* or *focus*.

An *epicenter* is the projection of a hypocenter onto the surface of the earth. *Tectonic plates* are the irregular plates that form the earth's crust. These plates are floating and constantly moving, and the movement of these plates is what primarily causes earthquakes. A *fault* is a boundary between tectonic plates.

59.   The answer is D.

The buildings that are best suited to the flat plate concrete deck system are those having relatively light live loads, such as residential buildings, motels, and so on. The answer is therefore choice D. Industrial and storage buildings have relatively large live loads, so choices A and B are incorrect. Office buildings generally have larger live loads than residential buildings, so choice C is also incorrect.

60.   The answer is B.

In a flat plate system, columns tend to punch through the slab due to the large shear stresses around the columns. This problem is known as the *punching shear*. To resist this shear, the slab can be made thicker around the columns by introducing a capital or a drop panel (concrete pad) on top of the columns.

61.   The answer is A.

The Richter scale is a logarithmic scale. An increase in magnitude of 1 corresponds to a tenfold increase in the amplitude of the seismic waves, or an increase of about 32 times in energy released. An increase in magnitude of 2 corresponds to a thousandfold increase in energy released. Thus, an earthquake of magnitude 6 on the Richter scale releases about 32 times more energy than an earthquake of magnitude 5.

62.   The answer is A.

A two-way concrete system is somewhat square in shape and reinforced for bending moment in both the short and long directions. The answer is therefore choice A. In the one-way slab, the reinforcement is placed for bending moment in the short direction, while the long direction is reinforced at a minimum ratio for temperature/shrinkage stresses.

63.   The answer is B.

A *waffle slab* is a slab that is ribbed in both directions (choice B).

A slab that is ribbed in one direction only is called a *pan joist* (choice A). Choices C and D are both incorrect because a waffle slab can be prestressed to span longer spans, but it does not have to be prestressed.

64.   The answer is D.

The building's fundamental period of vibration is directly proportional to the mass and inversely proportional to the stiffness. The period of vibration decreases with an increase in the building's stiffness and increases with an increase in the building's mass.

65.   The answer is C.

The function of stirrups in concrete beams is to resist the shear stresses that cannot be handled by the concrete alone (choice C). Stirrups are also referred to as *web reinforcement*.

66.   The answer is A.

The *pan joist* is a reinforced concrete slab system that is ribbed in one direction only. This system is strong compared to the other traditional concrete slab systems and is therefore best suited for buildings with heavy live loads, such as industrial and storage buildings (choice A). Hotels are similar to residential buildings in terms of live loads. Live loads are relatively light in these buildings, so choices B and C are incorrect. Live loads in office buildings are generally lower compared to the industrial and storage buildings, so choice D is also incorrect.

67.   The answer is D.

Prestressed concrete beams are used for long spans and heavy loads. They can span 100 ft (30 m) or more.

68.   The answer is D.

Structural systems can resist lateral forces by developing bending, shear, or axial tension and compression. Moment-resisting frames, which resist lateral loads by bending, constitute the least rigid system. A shear wall resists lateral forces by developing shear in its own plane and is the most rigid system. Braced frames are similar to a vertical truss and resist lateral forces by axial tension and compression in the members of the vertical truss.

69.   The answer is B.

The false statement about the dome of revolution is choice B. Bending in this system is minimal, and the stresses are direct compression or tension. All other statements are true.

70.   The answer is A.

Moment-resisting, or rigid, frames resist lateral forces by developing bending.

71.   The answer is B.

Shear walls can be constructed using reinforced concrete, reinforced masonry, steel, or wood stud walls. Unreinforced masonry should not be used to construct shear walls.

72.   The answer is D.

The hyperbolic paraboloid is the mathematical name given to the system created by twisting a plane surface. The name is used for a concrete shell with a double curvature (choice D). The system described in choice A is called a *barrel shell*. The system described in choice B is called a *short shell*. The concrete folded plate system in choice C is not a hyperbolic paraboloid.

73.   The answer is B.

The false statement about precast concrete is choice B. If a precast concrete element is prestressed, then it can be used for long spans and heavier loads. However, precast concrete elements are not always prestressed.

One of the main advantages of using precast concrete is the fast construction (choice A). Elements are precast and relatively quickly connected together on-site. The construction is also less affected by weather conditions.

Precast concrete is often produced under controlled factory conditions (choice C) and generally offers better quality control compared to sitecast concrete. Precast concrete, like regular concrete, has a high heat insulation value (choice D).

74.   The answer is C.

Based on the IBC, the base shear is given by

$$V = C_s W$$

C_s is the seismic response coefficient, and W is the effective seismic weight of the building.

The seismic response coefficient is given by

$$C_s = \frac{S_{DS}}{\dfrac{R}{I}}$$

S_{DS} is the design spectral response acceleration parameter in the short period range, R is the response modification factor, and I is the occupancy importance factor.

The value of the seismic response coefficient should satisfy some upper and lower limit conditions, and its value can be determined as follows.

The mapped spectral response values (S_s and S_1) for this site in Washington state are given as 0.50 and 0.15, respectively. Normally these values are taken from Figures 1613.5(1) and 1613.5(2) of the International Building Code (IBC).

These mapped spectral response values represent the amount of seismic risk and the intensity of the maximum considered earthquake based on the geographic location. The values on the map (50 and 15) are percents and must be divided by 100 when used in the design formulas, resulting in the value of 0.50 for S_s (which is the 0.2 sec spectral response acceleration) and of 0.15 for S_1 (the 1.0 sec spectral response acceleration). These mapped values are for site class B, which is the case in this problem. For other classes, these values must be adjusted for a specific site using the (F_a/F_v) factors as explained below.

Tables 8 and 9 can be used to determine the factors F_a and F_v for site class B. Based on these tables, the value is 1.0 for both factors.

According to the IBC, the design spectral response values are calculated as

$$S_{DS} = \tfrac{2}{3} F_a S_S = \left(\tfrac{2}{3}\right)(1.0)(0.50) = 0.33$$

$$S_{D1} = \tfrac{2}{3} F_v S_1 = \left(\tfrac{2}{3}\right)(1.0)(0.15) = 0.10$$

A residential building is classified as occupancy or use category II. (Table 7 in the Appendix describes the occupancy categories. It is not needed to solve this problem.)

The importance factor, I, is equal to 1.0 for occupancy categories I and II.

The response modification factor, R, is related to the type of structural system used and reflects the capability of various systems to absorb energy. Systems with a high ductility have higher R-values. The value of R is given as 4.

The values of the seismic response coefficient, C_s, can now be calculated.

$$C_s = \frac{S_{DS}}{\dfrac{R}{I}} = \frac{0.33}{\dfrac{4}{1.0}} = 0.083$$

The calculated value of C_s as 0.083 exceeds the given upper limit of 0.068 and is obviously higher than the lower limit of 0.01.

Based on these requirements, the value of C_s to consider is the upper limit of 0.068 or approximately 0.07.

The base shear, V, can now be determined by

$$V = C_s W = 0.07W$$

The base shear is about 7% of the effective seismic building weight in both U.S. units and SI units.

According to the ASCE/SEI 7 standard, the effective seismic building weight should include the total dead load along with other loads such as a minimum of 25% of the floor live load for areas used for storage, the actual partition weight or a minimum of 10 psf (0.48 kN/m²) of floor area (whichever is greater), the total operating weight of permanent equipment, and 20% of the uniform design snow load when the snow load exceeds 30 psf (1.44 kN/m²).

75.   The answer is D.

According to the ACI code, the maximum spacing between lateral ties of a reinforced concrete column should be the least of the following three dimensions: 16 times the reinforcing bar diameter, 48 times the tie diameter, or the least dimension of the column.

76.   The answer is D.

The correct statements are I, III, and IV. Torsional effects are most important in asymmetrical buildings such as buildings with L-configurations. These effects can be reduced by making both the building and its shear-resisting elements symmetrical and by placing the shear-resisting elements at the perimeter of the building. Shear walls and other vertical resisting systems that are of unequal rigidity or that are not symmetrical contribute to a torsional moment.

77.   The answer is D.

The tributary area of a typical interior column in this grid is 24 ft by 24 ft (7.3 m by 7.3 m) which is about 580 ft² (53 m²).

Choice B, 290 ft² (27 m²), is the approximate tributary area of a typical exterior column in this grid. This area would be 12 ft by 24 ft (3.65 m by 7.3 m).

78.   The answer is A, B, E, and F.

The IBC requires that a certain arbitrary amount of accidental torsion be considered in a design, even if the building is symmetrical, for all of the listed reasons except choices C and D.

The accidental torsion is not related to either the overturning moment or drift. The code requires that the mass at each level of the building be assumed to be displaced in each direction a distance equal to 5% of the building dimension at that level in the direction perpendicular to the direction of the force.

79.   The answer is D.

According to ACI code provisions for minimum slab thickness, the minimum overall thickness of a cantilevered slab of span L is $L/10$.

In U.S. units:

The minimum thickness, h, is

$$h = \frac{L}{10} = \left(\frac{11 \text{ ft}}{10}\right)\left(12 \frac{\text{in}}{\text{ft}}\right)$$

$$= 13 \text{ in}$$

In SI units:

The minimum thickness, h, is

$$h = \frac{L}{10} = \left(\frac{3.4 \text{ m}}{10}\right)\left(1000 \frac{\text{mm}}{\text{m}}\right)$$

$$= 340 \text{ mm}$$

Choices A, B, and C correspond to different support conditions of the slab.

80.   The answer is B.

The steel area is the product of the reinforcement ratio, ρ, the beam width, b, and the beam's effective depth, d.

$$A_s = \rho bd$$

In U.S. units:

The steel area is

$$A_s = (0.0142)(15 \text{ in})(22 \text{ in})$$

$$= 4.69 \text{ in}^2 \quad (4.7 \text{ in}^2)$$

In SI units:

The steel area is

$$A_s = (0.0142)(380 \text{ mm})(560 \text{ mm})$$

$$= 3020 \text{ mm}^2 \quad (3000 \text{ mm}^2)$$

81.   The answer is A, C, E, and F.

All the listed factors affect a building's response to an earthquake except for the local temperature and the orientation of the building. Other factors that have an effect are the quality of the construction and the distance from the epicenter of the quake.

82.   The answer is B.

In conventional construction, wood stud walls are built with studs that are generally spaced at 16 in (400) on center.

83.   The answer is A.

A steel stud wall is generally built using channel-shaped steel studs that are 2.5 in to 6 in deep (64 to 152) and spaced at 16 in (400) on center, as with wood stud walls.

84.   The answer is D.

The IBC requires that in seismic design categories D, E, and F, every building of more than six stories having an aggregate floor area of at least 60,000 ft² (5574 m²) and every building of 10 stories or more be provided with at least three accelerographs. These instruments must be placed in the basement, in the middle section, and near the top of the building.

A strong-motion accelerograph measures the acceleration of the ground or building during an earthquake. The ground does not move at a uniform velocity or speed during an earthquake. Acceleration is the rate of change in the velocity and is different from speed or velocity.

Strong-motion accelerographs normally stop working when subject to strong ground motion. They are activated by the earthquake, record the earth motion, and then stop working. The acceleration is measured as a percentage of gravitational acceleration g. Their records provide important information for research and building design.

85. The answer is B.

Masonry is like concrete: strong in compression and weak in tension.

86. The answer is B.

A diaphragm is considered flexible when the maximum lateral deformation is more than twice the average story drift of the story it's designed for.

87. The answer is C.

Exterior columns used with tilt-up walls do not necessarily have to be precast concrete. These columns can also be cast-in-place concrete or steel columns.

88. The answer is A.

In a flexible diaphragm, lateral loads are transferred to the vertical resisting elements according to tributary area. In a rigid diaphragm, the lateral loads are transferred to the vertical resisting elements in proportion to the relative stiffness of these elements.

The *rigidity* of a wall is its resistance to deformation. In a flexible diaphragm, the rigidity of the walls is not considered. For instance, for a flexible diaphragm supported on two end walls and a central wall, the central wall, which has a tributary area equal to twice the tributary area of the end wall, will resist an amount of lateral load equal to twice the lateral load resisted by an end wall. This means that the central wall will pick up half of the total lateral load, while each end wall resists only a quarter of this load.

The tributary area concept is not used in the case of the rigid diaphragm. In this type of diaphragm, the lateral load is distributed to the walls in proportion to rigidity. A wall that is twice as rigid as another will resist twice the lateral load resisted by the wall of lower rigidity.

89. The answer is A.

A *mat foundation* is one large footing that covers an entire floor area. It is normally used when the soil's load-bearing capacity is low, requiring large footings and causing the total column footing area to be relatively large compared to the floor plan. A mat foundation replaces the individual footings with one large footing that covers the entire floor plan.

A footing used for two close columns is called a *combined footing*, so choice B is incorrect. A mat foundation is not a pile, so choice C is also incorrect. The slab described in choice D is called a *pile cap*, which is very different from a mat foundation.

90. The answer is B.

The square floor plan (choice B) is the best shape for lateral loads. The figures in choices A (L-shaped), C (U-shaped), and D (cross-shaped) show floor plans with reentrant corners, which should be avoided when possible. If reentrant corners cannot be avoided, then drag struts or seismic separations must be considered.

91. The answer is B.

A raft, or compensated, footing is a mat foundation that is placed deep in the soil so that the weight of the excavated soil is about equal to the weight of the building.

92. The answer is A.

A soil's load-bearing capacity increases with depth, so choices B and C are incorrect. Choice D is also incorrect. It is true that a soil's load-bearing capacity is related to the soil type; for instance, sedimentary rocks can carry more loads than clay. However, in a given soil, the bearing capacity will also increase with depth, and therefore the type of soil is not the only factor affecting a soil's bearing capacity.

93. The answer is B.

The problematic building elevation is shown in choice B. This configuration is unstable because the weight of the building is resting on a base that is smaller than the rest of the structure.

An opposite design is shown in choice D. Here the base of the building is wider than the top, which helps with the general stability of the building. Choice A is regular in shape, and no problems are to be expected with it. In choice C, the building is supported on columns, which suggests a soft story; however the columns are braced as shown, which constitutes an acceptable design practice.

One of the most important design recommendations for lateral loads is regularity. Buildings and structures must be regular in stiffness and shape both in plan and in vertical configuration. Symmetry is another good rule of design, as it helps in the general structural stability of a building. Reentrant corners as well as sudden changes in shape or stiffness must be avoided. In a vertical configuration, pyramidal shapes should have the wide side at the base. The load path must always be continuous, and the lateral load-resisting elements should not be interrupted.

94.   The answer is D.

Timber piles have the lowest initial cost and least load-bearing capacity. The general depth range of these piles is 25 ft to 40 ft (7.6 m to 12.2 m). Their safe load-bearing capacity varies from 30 kip to 80 kip (133 kN to 356 kN).

95.   The answer is A.

Reentrant corners create some problems under lateral loads and it is better to avoid them, but building codes do not forbid them.

If reentrant corners cannot be avoided, then the best solution is to provide a seismic separation. Another solution is to use drag struts to help transfer lateral loads properly.

96.   The answer is B.

For depths between 10 ft and 20 ft (3 m and 6 m), the most efficient retaining wall type would be the cantilever wall. A gravity wall is not economical beyond a depth of about 4 ft (1.2 m). A counterfort wall is a stronger retaining wall that is generally used for depths of about 25 ft (7.6 m) or more.

97.   The answer is A.

Adding a shear key to the base of a cantilever retaining wall helps prevent sliding of the wall by increasing the contact surface, and therefore the frictional forces, between the base of the wall and the soil.

98.   The answer is C.

Base isolation can be applied to both new and existing structures. Los Angeles City Hall, which dates back to the 1920s, was placed on base isolators during a renovation completed in 2001. This building sits on a fault line, which makes it vulnerable to earthquakes. Engineers chose to lift this building and place it on base isolators to help protect it from seismic forces.

An example of a new building placed on base isolators is the International Terminal at San Francisco International Airport, which opened in late 2000. This terminal, the centerpiece of a $2.6 billion expansion and modernization program, incorporates 267 friction-pendulum cast-steel base isolators. The isolators were installed at the feet of structural columns, allowing a lateral displacement of up to 20 in (510). The terminal is one of the largest structures built on base isolators.

99.   The answer is A.

According to the IBC, a *soft story* is a story in which the lateral stiffness is less than 70% of that in the story above or less than 80% of the average stiffness of the stories above.

Choice B describes an *extremely soft story*. Choice D describes a *weak story*. Choice C does not correspond to any story type as defined in the IBC.

100.   The answer is B.

Before building the Eiffel Tower, French engineer Gustave Eiffel was best known for his iron bridges. Eiffel built bridges in Portugal, Peru, Algeria, and China as well as countless viaducts and railway bridges in Europe. At the age of 25, he was put in charge of the construction of a bridge over the Garonne River at Bordeaux in France, one of the largest iron structures of its day. Eiffel adopted a new method of pile-driving there, and his success in completing the bridge on schedule helped establish his name.

Eiffel is also known for building a harbor in Chile, churches in Peru and the Philippines, a dam in France, the Bon Marché department store in Paris, and many other projects. His designs for lock gates for the Panama Canal were ultimately not used when the United States took over the failing French efforts. Eiffel also published a formula for calculating stresses and strains. The structures he designed are strong and economical, and lightness is evident in his designs.

101.   The answer is A.

The Italian contractor and engineer Pier Luigi Nervi is known primarily for his concrete domes and concrete shell roofs, including two domes at the Rome Olympic Games Complex, and some aircraft hangars with concrete shell roofs. The smaller dome of the Rome Olympic Games Complex, the Palazetto dello Sport, was built in the late 1950s and used prestressed concrete.

102.   The answer is C.

The earthquake effects or damages not covered in the building codes are landslides, soil liquefaction, and avalanches (II, III, and IV). Building codes cover ground shaking or vibration effects. Vibration generally covers a large area and can occur in any direction, including the vertical direction. The current practice, however, is to consider only the horizontal or lateral movement; the vertical component of the vibration is ignored since the component is small compared to the horizontal component, and the weight of the building tends to counterbalance the vertical forces.

103. The answer is D.

The most flexible lateral load resisting system uses moment-resisting frames. This system resists lateral loads by bending and flexure in the members. Joints are designed to be rigid, and bending generally occurs in the beam and column components of the frame.

The IBC classifies the moment-resisting frames into three types: special moment-resisting frames, intermediate moment-resisting frames, and ordinary moment-resisting frames, depending on the restrictive requirements.

104. The answer is C.

The name of the structural engineer who designed both the Sears Tower and the John Hancock Building in Chicago is Fazlur Kahn. Kahn was a partner in the firm of Skidmore, Owings, and Merrill and was a prominent structural engineer. He was one of the pioneers of tubular design in high-rise construction, which was developed in the 1960s.

105. The answer is D.

Intermediate moment-resisting frames are generally not permitted in seismic design categories D, E, or F. However, steel intermediate moment-resisting frames with heights up to 35 ft (11 m) can be used in category D. The design requirements of the intermediate moment-resisting frames are less stringent compared to the special moment-resisting frames. The latter type must be ductile and must satisfy certain provisions of the IBC.

106. The answer is D.

William Le Baron Jenney designed the first steel-framed building in the United States, which is the Home Life Insurance Building in Chicago. Prior to the development of the steel frame, the loads in a building were carried mainly by heavy masonry walls. These walls became thicker with the increase in the building height, which prompted the need for a new system, leading to the concept of the steel frame. In this concept, the loads are carried by a steel frame or skeleton of beams, girders, and columns, and the walls are not loadbearing.

107. The answer is A.

In the dual system, the moment-resisting frame must be able to resist at least 25% of the base shear.

A dual system is basically a structural system with two components. A complete frame system supports the gravity dead and live loads, and a specially detailed moment-resisting frame and shear walls or braced frames resist the lateral loads. The moment-resisting frame must resist at least 25% of the base shear. The moment-resisting frame can be built using steel or concrete.

108. The answer is A.

The Yale University Skating Rink designed by Eero Saarinen is an example of a cable roof structure. The steel cables are connected to a central reinforced concrete arch on one side and are anchored to heavy, curved concrete walls on the other side. They support a wooden roof.

109. The answer is C.

The thickness of the concrete walls supporting the dome of the Pantheon in Rome is approximately 20 ft. The Pantheon is the largest dome of antiquity. It was built by the emperor Hadrian in A.D. 123. The Romans used concrete to build this dome. The dome has a 24 ft thick circular foundation wall, and it sits on top of 20 ft thick support walls. It spans about 142 ft internally.

110. The answer is 50.

According to the IBC, a plan structural irregularity can be caused by large openings when the total open area exceeds 50% of the gross enclosed diaphragm area. This is known in the IBC as a *diaphragm discontinuity*. According to the IBC, a diaphragm discontinuity could also be due to diaphragms with abrupt discontinuities or variations in stiffness, or changes in effective diaphragm stiffness of more than 50% from one story to the next.

111. The answer is D.

The main materials used to build the Crystal Palace in London were glass with cast and wrought iron. The Crystal Palace had about 4500 tons (4100 metric tons) of cast and wrought iron and about 900,000 ft^2 (84 000 m^2) of sheet glass. The structure also used wood for the mullions and interior arches. The Palace looked like a greenhouse and consisted mainly of iron columns and glass-covered roof trusses. The Crystal Palace was built in 1851 for the first World's Fair and for the Great Exhibition of the Works of Industry of All Nations. It covered 19 acres of London's Hyde Park and later became an inspiration for other exhibition halls and arcades. It also started a trend in prefabricated modular construction.

112. The answer is C.

According to the IBC, the period, T, is given by

$$T = C_U T_a$$

The coefficient for the upper limit on the calculated period, C_U, is taken from Table 2.7. For the design spectral response acceleration parameter at 1 sec, S_{D1}, given as 0.15, the coefficient C_U is 1.6. T_a is the approximate period of vibration. Substituting in the previous equation,

$$T = (1.6)(0.40 \text{ sec}) = 0.64 \text{ sec}$$

113. The answer is A.

The structural engineer who designed the tent of the Munich Olympic Stadium in Germany is Frei Otto. The stadium is a remarkable structure consisting of a tent made of acrylic glass supported on a network of cables that are in turn supported by steel masts placed on the outer periphery of the stadium (so that the masts do not obstruct viewer sightlines). The masts are anchored to the ground using guy ropes.

114. The answer is D.

To minimize the risk of pounding, a seismic separation must be provided between the two adjacent buildings, and it should be equal to the sum of the expected drifts of the two buildings, modified by a safety factor.

115. The answer is D.

In cast-in-place concrete construction, more than 50% of the total construction costs is related to the formwork. Therefore, a maximum reuse of formwork in concrete construction is an important factor for economy.

116. The answer is B.

The correct and most practical solution is to provide a moment-resisting frame in the front. The rear is rigid and the front is open, so it is flexible. Providing a moment-resisting frame in the front will make the front as rigid as possible while maintaining the possibility of an opening there.

Drag struts will not solve the problem in this case; therefore A is incorrect. Increasing the safety factors in the design calculations is not a solution. Safety factors are normally given by building codes; designers do not select their own factors. Also, increasing the safety factors does not resolve the irregularity resulting from a flexible front and a rigid rear. Changing the entire design and eliminating the opening would generally not be a practical solution, so choice D is incorrect.

117. The answer is A.

The approximate period of vibration is

$$T_a = C_t h_n^x$$

h_n is the building height above the base to the highest point. C_t and x are the approximate period parameters and are given in Table 6. These parameters depend on the structure type. A bearing wall system with reinforced concrete walls falls in the category of "all other structural systems" on the table. Therefore, the coefficient C_t is 0.02 when U.S. units are used and 0.0488 when SI units are used. The value of x is 0.75 for both unit systems.

In U.S. units:

$$T_a = C_t h_n^x$$
$$= (0.02)(24 \text{ ft})^{0.75}$$
$$= 0.22 \text{ sec}$$

In SI units:

$$T_a = C_t h_n^x$$
$$= (0.0488)(7.3 \text{ m})^{0.75}$$
$$= 0.22 \text{ s}$$

118. The answer is B.

In a typical building, such as a traditional office building, the actual cost of the structure represents about 25% to 30% of the total construction cost. The rest is divided between mechanical, electrical, interior finishes, fixtures, ceilings, and hardware. The mechanical and electrical systems represent about 20% to 30% of the total construction cost. These proportions are not applicable to high-rise buildings and long-span structures where the structural system becomes the most important component.

119. The answer is A.

A36 steel is not normally used in the manufacture of bolts for steel connections; instead, high-strength steels are generally used. High-strength steels include the three other types listed in the problem: A325, A490, and A449, all of which have a yield stress of 85 ksi or higher. A36 steel, with a yield stress of 36 ksi or a little more, can be used in the manufacture of the threaded parts and is generally used for beams, columns, and other structural shapes.

120. The answer is B.

The moment, M, of a force, F, is equal to the force multiplied by the length of the arm, d.

$$M = Fd$$

The seismic load is uniformly distributed on the parapet wall, so first the resultant of this uniform load must be calculated by multiplying the uniform load by the area using a unit width of the parapet wall. This resultant is then considered to be acting at midheight of the parapet, which means that the arm of this resultant is one-half of the parapet height.

In U.S. units:

The seismic load of the parapet is given as 48 psf.

The resultant of the seismic uniform load, per foot of width of the parapet, is

$$R = Phw = \left(48 \frac{\text{lbf}}{\text{ft}^2}\right)(4 \text{ ft})(1 \text{ ft}) = 192 \text{ lbf}$$

The moment of this resultant (again per foot of parapet width) is

$$M = Rd = R\left(\frac{h}{2}\right)$$

$$= (192 \text{ lbf})\left(\frac{4 \text{ ft}}{2}\right)$$

$$= 384 \text{ ft-lbf} \quad (380 \text{ ft-lbf})$$

In SI units:

The seismic load of the parapet is

$$P = (2.3 \text{ kPa})\left(1000 \frac{\text{Pa}}{\text{kPa}}\right)$$

$$= 2300 \text{ Pa} \quad (2300 \text{ N/m}^2)$$

The resultant of the seismic uniform load, per meter of width of the parapet, is

$$R = Phw = \left(2300 \frac{\text{N}}{\text{m}^2}\right)(1.2 \text{ m})(1 \text{ m}) = 2760 \text{ N}$$

The moment of this resultant (again per meter of parapet width) is

$$M = Rd = R\left(\frac{h}{2}\right)$$

$$= (2760 \text{ N})\left(\frac{1.2 \text{ m}}{2}\right)$$

$$= 1656 \text{ N·m} \quad (1700 \text{ N·m})$$

121. The answer is C.

This is a bearing-type double-shear connection. The bolt value must be determined both in shear and in bearing, and it must be multiplied by the number of bolts. The lower value controls and must be used as the allowable load for this connection.

To determine the bolt value in shear, use Table 2. On this table, next to "bolts" and under "ASTM designation", select the steel type A325.

Under "connection type", select N for a bearing-type connection with threads included in shear plane. Under "hole type", select STD for a standard round hole. Under "loading", select D for double shear. On the top row, under "nominal diameter", select the diameter of the bolt as $^7/_8$ in. Read the corresponding bolt value in shear. This value, 25.3 kips, is the allowable capacity of one bolt. For three bolts, multiply this by 3.

$$(3)(25.3 \text{ kips}) = 75.9 \text{ kips}$$

To determine the bolt value in bearing, use Table 14.

The total thickness of the single plate in one direction is $^1/_2$ in. The total thickness of the two plates in the other direction is

$$(2)\left(\frac{3}{8} \text{ in}\right) = \frac{3}{4} \text{ in}$$

The smaller thickness of $^1/_2$ in controls the design.

From Table 14, under "material thickness", select a thickness of $^1/_2$ in. On the top row, select the tensile strength of the steel given in the problem as 58 ksi, then select the bolt diameter of $^7/_8$ in. Read the bolt value in bearing, which is 30.5 kips. For three bolts, the total value is

$$(3)(30.5 \text{ kips}) = 91.5 \text{ kips}$$

Compare the shear capacity of 75.9 kips to the bearing capacity of 91.5 kips. The lower value governs the design, and therefore the allowable load for this connection is 75.9 kips.

122. The answer is D.

On average, about 1000 tornadoes are reported in the United States each year. However, only a few are rated violent (F-4 or F-5 on the Fujita scale).

Tornadoes can be defined as inverted cloud cores consisting of a violent, rotating column of air. They are complex wind events that can cause various levels of devastation. Tornadoes are smaller than hurricanes but have greater wind speeds. The inventor of the Fujita scale, Tetsuya Theodore Fujita, estimated that only 1% of the total area within a violent tornado's path experiences damage related to violent wind speeds. The typical rotational speed of a tornado is estimated to be about 250 mph (400 km/h), but speeds can sometimes exceed 500 mph (800 km/h).

123. The answer is 12.

Since the truss and the loading are symmetrical, there is no need to write the static equations of equilibrium for this truss. The support reactions are equal, and each reaction is equal to one half of the total load applied on the truss.

$$R_A = R_D = \frac{15 + 15}{2} = 15$$

The method of sections can be used to find the force in the member EF. Make a section through the members EF, EC, and BC, which will divide the truss into two parts. Choose one side of the truss and draw a free-body diagram for this side showing all forces acting on it, including the internal forces in the members that are cut. The three unknown internal forces inside the members EF, EC, and BC can be found by writing and solving the three static equations of equilibrium for this side of the truss. Since the problem asks for the force in the member EF only, one equation of equilibrium is sufficient.

Choosing the left side of the truss, the sum of the moments about joint C can be written. The sum of all moments there should be zero. Choosing the joint C for the summation of moments would eliminate the moments of all forces passing through C from the equation because these forces have a zero arm there.

In U.S. units:

Because $\Sigma M_C = 0$, the force in member EF is

$$F_{EF}(15 \text{ ft}) - (15 \text{ kips})(12 \text{ ft}) =$$

$$F_{EF} = \frac{(15 \text{ kips})(12 \text{ ft})}{15 \text{ ft}}$$

$$= 12 \text{ kips}$$

In SI units:

Because $\Sigma M_C = 0$, the force in member EF is

$$F_{EF}(5 \text{ m}) - (15 \text{ kN})(4 \text{ m}) = 0$$

$$F_{EF} = \frac{(15 \text{ kN})(4 \text{ m})}{5 \text{ m}}$$

$$= 12 \text{ kN}$$

124. The answer is C.

The 1906 San Francisco earthquake hit at 5:12 A.M. on Wednesday, April 18. Its magnitude on the Richter scale is usually given as 8.3, but other values have been proposed, generally ranging from 7.7 to 8.3.

The epicenter of the earthquake was about 2 mi (3 km) offshore. It ruptured a 296 mi (477 km) long stretch of the San Andreas Fault. The strong shaking, which lasted 45 to 60 seconds, was felt as far away as Los Angeles, southern Oregon, and central Nevada.

The earthquake caused a fire that raged for three days, destroying almost all of San Francisco's downtown and much of its residential area. The number of deaths caused by the earthquake and resulting fires has often been given as 700, but this number is now believed to be 3000 or more. More than half of San Francisco's 410,000 people were left homeless. The damage was estimated at the time to be about $400 million.

An extensive study of the 1906 San Francisco earthquake, published in two parts in 1908 and 1910, was led by geologist Andrew Lawson of the University of California. The Lawson Report was the first to establish that earthquakes were not random events but caused by the buildup of stresses along an active fault. The report marked the beginning of the science of seismology in the United States, and is still the most important study of any single earthquake.

125. The answer is B.

According to the IBC, the equivalent lateral force method can always be used in seismic design categories A, B, and C. The method may also be used for buildings in categories D, E, and F if they are

- regular structures with $T < 3.5T_s$

- irregular structures with $T < 3.5T_s$, with plan irregularities 2, 3, 4, or 5 only, or vertical irregularities 4 or 5

T is the fundamental period of vibration. T_s is the ratio S_{D1}/S_{DS}. (These variables are explained in the solution to problem 46.)

Plan irregularities 2, 3, 4, and 5 are reentrant corners, diaphragm discontinuity, out-of-plane offsets, and nonparallel systems, respectively. Vertical irregularities 4 and 5 are, respectively, in-plane discontinuity in vertical lateral-force resisting elements and discontinuity in capacity (weak story).

All other structures should be designed with the dynamic method of analysis.

PRACTICE EXAM: VIGNETTE SOLUTIONS

STRUCTURAL LAYOUT: PASSING SOLUTION

This vignette requires the candidate to lay out a basic structural concept for a small building by placing columns, bearing walls, steel joists, and decking. The problem includes a building with two different roof heights and various types of openings.

Lower Roof Framing

The lower roof is supported on steel joists and metal decking. The joist spacing at 5 ft (1525) on center is within the program limits. The south wall and the wall separating the sewing area from the rest of the building are designated as load-bearing walls, and the joists are spanning perpendicular to these walls and are supported mainly by them. The east-west walls at the ends of the lower roof area need not be load-bearing. Joists drawn at these ends compensate for the lack of load-bearing walls there. Lintels are provided at all doorways and window openings in the load-bearing walls.

Upper Roof Framing

The upper roof area is also supported on steel joists and metal decking. Again, joist spacing at 5 ft (1525) on center is within the limits of the program. The north wall and the wall separating the sewing area from the rest of the building are designated as load-bearing walls, and the joists are directly supported by them. The four columns shown are supported on the load-bearing wall between the sewing area and the other side of the building. The steel beams supported on these columns accommodate the clerestory window located along the full length of this wall.

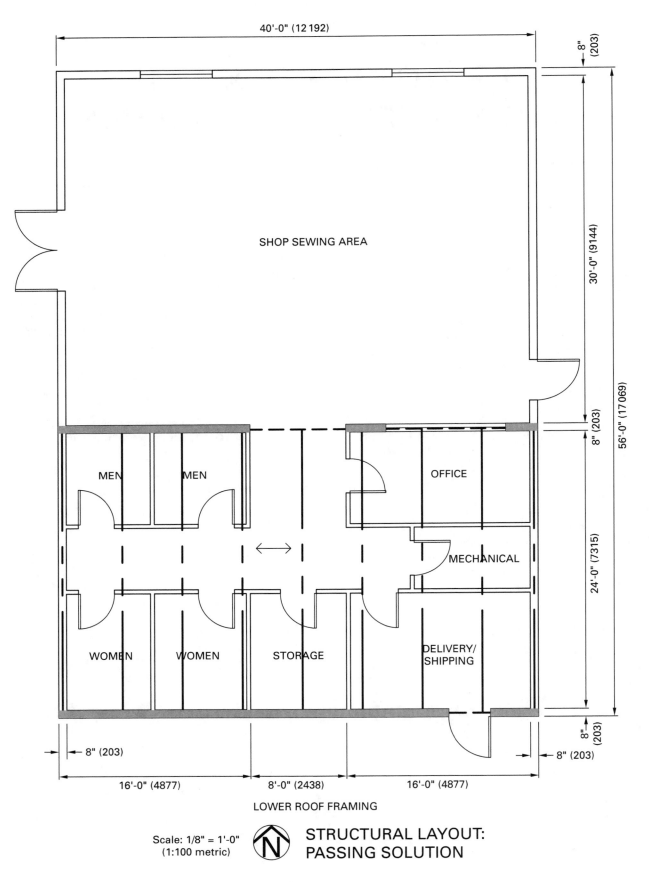

40'-0" (12 192)

8" (203)

SHOP SEWING AREA

30'-0" (9144)

56'-0" (17 069)

8" (203)

MEN   MEN

OFFICE

MECHANICAL

24'-0" (7315)

WOMEN   WOMEN   STORAGE

DELIVERY/
SHIPPING

8" (203)

8" (203)

8" (203)

16'-0" (4877)   8'-0" (2438)   16'-0" (4877)

LOWER ROOF FRAMING

Scale: 1/8" = 1'-0"
(1:100 metric)

**STRUCTURAL LAYOUT:
PASSING SOLUTION**

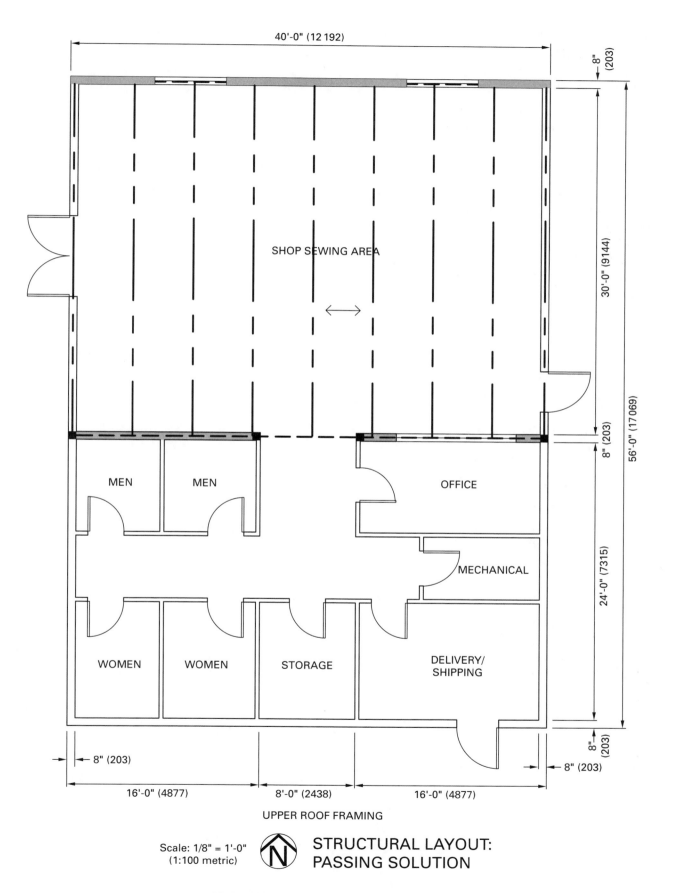

40'-0" (12 192)

8" (203)

8" (203)

30'-0" (9144)

56'-0" (17 069)

SHOP SEWING AREA

⟷

8" (203)

MEN

MEN

OFFICE

MECHANICAL

24'-0" (7315)

WOMEN

WOMEN

STORAGE

DELIVERY/
SHIPPING

8" (203)

8" (203)

8" (203)

16'-0" (4877)

8'-0" (2438)

16'-0" (4877)

UPPER ROOF FRAMING

Scale: 1/8" = 1'-0"
(1:100 metric)

STRUCTURAL LAYOUT:
PASSING SOLUTION

STRUCTURAL LAYOUT: FAILING SOLUTION

Lower Roof Framing

The framing in this solution does not meet the program requirements. The joist spacing drawn at 6 ft (1830) on center exceeds the limits of the program.

Upper Roof Framing

Again, the joist spacing drawn at 6 ft (1830) on center exceeds the limits of the program. The designation of the load-bearing walls is modified compared to the lower roof framing plan, and the joists span the longer 40 ft (12 192) direction. The arrows that should be used to indicate the direction of the decking are missing.

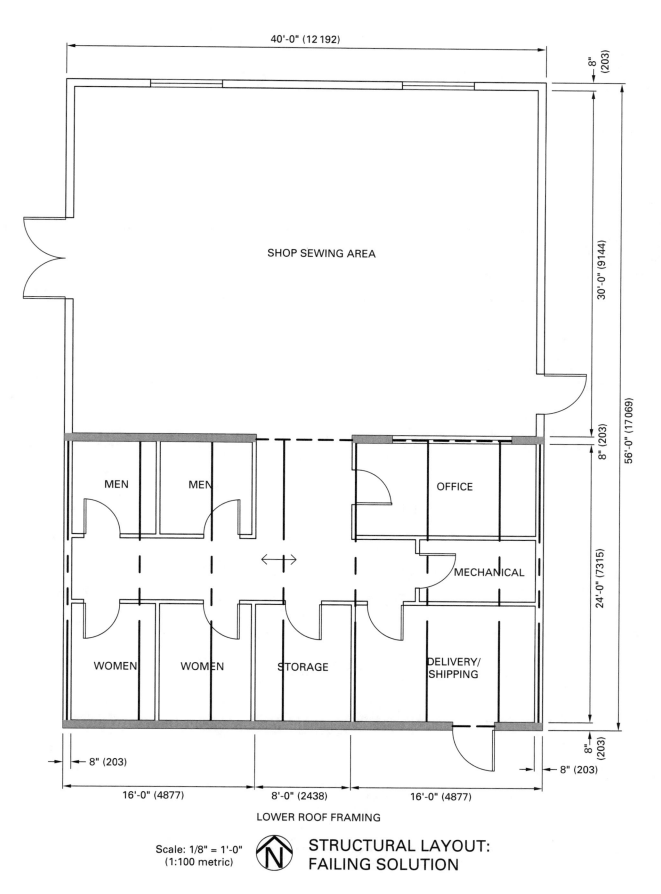

LOWER ROOF FRAMING

Scale: 1/8" = 1'-0"
(1:100 metric)

STRUCTURAL LAYOUT:
FAILING SOLUTION

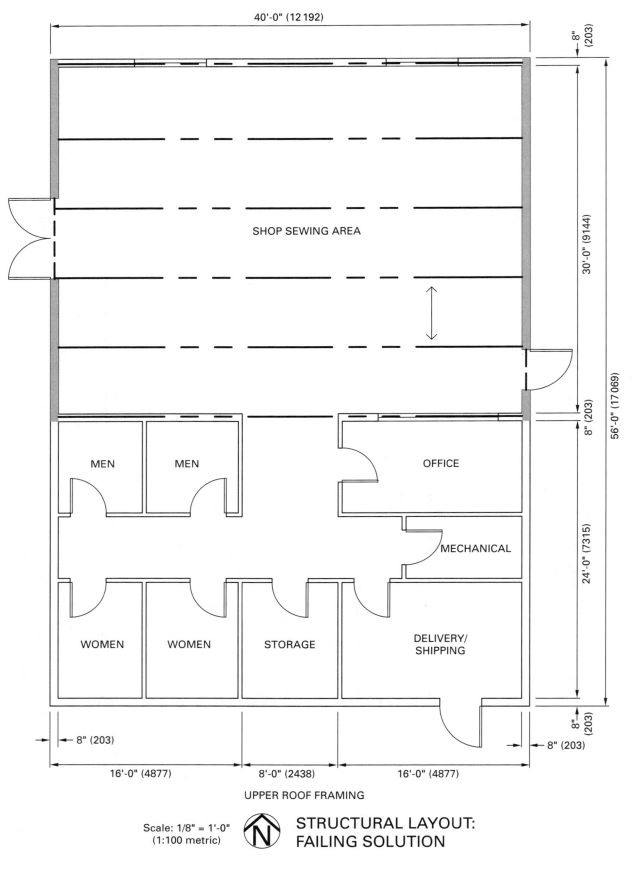

40'-0" (12 192)

8" (203)

SHOP SEWING AREA

30'-0" (9144)

56'-0" (17 069)

8" (203)

MEN   MEN   OFFICE

MECHANICAL

24'-0" (7315)

WOMEN   WOMEN   STORAGE   DELIVERY/
SHIPPING

8" (203)

8" (203)   8" (203)

16'-0" (4877)   8'-0" (2438)   16'-0" (4877)

UPPER ROOF FRAMING

Scale: 1/8" = 1'-0"   (N)   STRUCTURAL LAYOUT:
(1:100 metric)   FAILING SOLUTION

APPENDIX:
FIGURES AND TABLES

Figure 1
Basic Wind Speed
in miles per hour (meters per second)

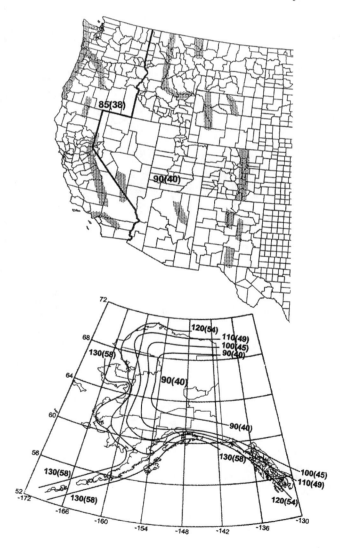

Reproduced from the 2005 edition of the ASCE/SEI 7 standard,
Minimum Design Loads for Buildings and Other Structures,
with permission from the publisher,
the American Society of Civil Engineers.

Table 1
Section Properties of Standard Dressed (S4S) Sawn Lumber

nominal size $b \times d$	standard dressed size (SDS) $b \times d$ (in $\times$ in)	area of section A (in²)	X-X axis		Y-Y axis	
			section modulus S_{xx} (in³)	moment of inertia I_{xx} (in⁴)	section modulus S_{yy} (in³)	moment of inertia I_{yy} (in⁴)
1 × 3	³/₄ × 2¹/₂	1.875	0.781	0.977	0.234	0.088
1 × 4	³/₄ × 3¹/₂	2.625	1.531	2.680	0.328	0.123
1 × 6	³/₄ × 5¹/₂	4.125	3.781	10.40	0.516	0.193
1 × 8	³/₄ × 7¹/₄	5.438	6.570	23.82	0.680	0.255
1 × 10	³/₄ × 9¹/₄	6.938	10.70	49.47	0.867	0.325
1 × 12	³/₄ × 11¹/₄	8.438	15.82	88.99	1.055	0.396
2 × 3	1¹/₂ × 2¹/₂	3.750	1.563	1.953	0.938	0.703
2 × 4	1¹/₂ × 3¹/₂	5.250	3.063	5.359	1.313	0.984
2 × 5	1¹/₂ × 4¹/₂	6.750	5.063	11.39	1.688	1.266
2 × 6	1¹/₂ × 5¹/₂	8.250	7.563	20.80	2.063	1.547
2 × 8	1¹/₂ × 7¹/₄	10.88	13.14	47.63	2.719	2.039
2 × 10	1¹/₂ × 9¹/₄	13.88	21.39	98.93	3.469	2.602
2 × 12	1¹/₂ × 11¹/₄	16.88	31.64	178.0	4.219	3.164
2 × 14	1¹/₂ × 13¹/₄	19.88	43.89	290.8	4.969	3.727
3 × 4	2¹/₂ × 3¹/₂	8.750	5.104	8.932	3.646	4.557
3 × 5	2¹/₂ × 4¹/₂	11.25	8.438	18.98	4.668	5.859
3 × 6	2¹/₂ × 5¹/₂	13.75	12.60	34.66	5.729	7.161
3 × 8	2¹/₂ × 7¹/₄	18.13	21.90	79.39	7.552	9.440
3 × 10	2¹/₂ × 9¹/₄	23.13	35.65	164.9	9.635	12.04
3 × 12	2¹/₂ × 11¹/₄	28.13	52.73	296.6	11.72	14.65
3 × 14	2¹/₂ × 13¹/₄	33.13	73.15	484.6	13.80	17.25
3 × 16	2¹/₂ × 15¹/₄	38.13	96.90	738.9	15.89	19.86

Adapted from the *Supplement to the 2005 National Design Specification®: Design Values for Wood Construction*, courtesy, American Forest & Paper Association, Washington, DC.

Table 2
Shear Bolt Values
Allowable Loads (in kips)

ASTM designation		connection type[1]	hole type[2]	F_v (ksi)	loading[3]	nominal diameter d (in)							
						$^5/_8$	$^3/_4$	$^7/_8$	1	$1^1/_8$	$1^1/_4$	$1^3/_8$	$1^1/_2$
						area, based on nominal diameter (in²)							
						0.3068	0.4418	0.6013	0.7854	0.9940	1.227	1.485	1.767
bolts	A307	–	STD, NSL	10.0	S	3.1	4.4	6.0	7.9	9.9	12.3	14.8	17.7
					D	6.1	8.8	12.0	15.7	19.9	24.5	29.7	35.3
	A325	SC class A	STD	17.0	S	5.22	7.51	10.2	13.4	16.9	20.9	25.2	30.0
					D	10.4	15.0	20.4	26.7	33.8	41.7	50.5	60.1
			OVS, SSL	15.0	S	4.60	6.63	9.02	11.8	14.9	18.4	22.3	26.5
					D	9.20	13.3	18.0	23.6	29.8	36.8	44.6	53.0
			LSL	12.0	S	3.68	5.30	7.22	9.42	11.9	14.7	17.8	21.2
					D	7.36	10.6	14.4	18.8	23.9	29.4	35.6	42.4
		N	STD, NSL	21.0	S	6.4	9.3	12.6	16.5	20.9	25.8	31.2	37.1
					D	12.9	18.6	25.3	33.0	41.7	51.5	62.4	74.2
		X	STD, NSL	30.0	S	9.2	13.3	18.0	23.6	29.8	36.8	44.5	53.0
					D	18.4	26.5	36.1	47.1	59.6	73.6	89.1	106.0
	A490	SC class A	STD	21.0	S	6.44	9.28	12.6	16.5	20.9	25.8	31.2	37.1
					D	12.9	18.6	25.3	33.0	41.7	51.5	62.4	74.2
			OVS, SSL	18.0	S	5.52	7.95	10.8	14.1	17.9	22.1	26.7	31.8
					D	11.0	15.9	21.6	28.3	35.8	44.2	53.5	63.6
			LSL	15.0	S	4.60	6.63	9.02	11.8	14.9	18.4	22.3	26.5
					D	9.20	13.3	18.0	23.6	29.8	36.8	44.6	53.0
		N	STD, NSL	28.0	S	8.6	12.4	16.8	22.0	27.8	34.4	41.6	49.5
					D	17.2	24.7	33.7	44.0	55.7	68.7	83.2	99.0
		X	STD, NSL	40.0	S	12.3	17.7	24.1	31.4	39.8	49.1	59.4	70.7
					D	24.5	35.3	48.1	62.8	79.5	98.2	119.0	141.0

[1]SC: slip critical connection
 N: bearing-type connection with threads *included* in shear plane
 X: bearing-type connection with threads *excluded* from shear plane
[2]STD: standard round holes ($d + ^1/_{16}$ in)
 LSL: long-slotted holes normal to load direction
 NSL: long- or short-slotted holes normal to load direction
 OVS: oversize round holes
 SSL: short-slotted holes
[3]S: single shear
 D: double shear

Table 3

Seismic Design Category Based on
Short-Period Response Accelerations

value of S_{DS}	occupancy category		
	I or II	II	III
$S_{DS} \leq 0.167g$	A	A	A
$0.167g \leq S_{DS} < 0.33g$	B	B	C
$0.33g \leq S_{DS} < 0.50g$	C	C	D
$0.50g \leq S_{DS}$	D	D	D

Adapted with permission from the 2006 International
Building Code. Copyright 2006. Washington, DC:
International Code Council, Inc.

Table 4

Seismic Design Category Based on
1-Second Response Accelerations

value of S_{D1}	occupancy category		
	I or II	II	III
$S_{D1} < 0.067g$	A	A	A
$0.067g \leq S_{D1} < 0.133g$	B	B	C
$0.133g \leq S_{D1} < 0.20g$	C	C	D
$0.20g \leq S_{D1}$	D	D	D

Adapted with permission from the 2006 International
Building Code. Copyright 2006. Washington, DC:
International Code Council, Inc.

Table 5

Coefficient for Upper Limit on Calculated Period

design spectral response acceleration parameter at 1 s, S_{D1}	coefficient C_u
≥ 0.4	1.4
0.3	1.4
0.2	1.5
0.15	1.6
≤ 0.1	1.7

Adapted from the 2005 edition of the ASCE/SEI 7 standard,
Minimum Design Loads for Buildings and Other Structures,
with permission from the publisher,
the American Society of Civil Engineers.

Table 6

Values of Approximate Period Parameters C_t and x

moment-resisting frame systems in which the frames resist 100% of the required seismic force and are not enclosed or adjoined by components that are more rigid and will prevent the frames from deflecting where subjected to seismic forces:	C_t	x
steel moment-resisting frames	0.028 (0.0724)	0.8
concrete moment-resisting frames	0.016 (0.0466)	0.9
eccentrically braced steel frames	0.03 (0.0731)	0.75
all other structural systems	0.02 (0.0488)	0.75

Metric equivalents are shown in parentheses.

Reproduced from the 2005 edition of the ASCE/SEI 7 standard,
Minimum Design Loads for Buildings and Other Structures,
with permission from the publisher,
the American Society of Civil Engineers.

Table 7
Occupancy Category of Buildings and Other Structures

occupancy category	nature of occupancy
I	buildings and other structures that represent a low hazard to human life in the event of failure, including but not limited to • agricultural facilities • certain temporary facilities • minor storage facilities
II	buildings and other structures except those listed in occupancy categories I, III, and IV
III	buildings and other structures that represent a substantial hazard to human life in the event of failure, including but not limited to • covered structures whose primary occupancy is public assembly with an occupant load greater than 300 • buildings and other structures with elementary school, secondary school, or day care facilities with an occupant load greater than 250 • buildings and other structures with an occupant load greater than 500 for colleges or adult eduction facilities • jails and detention facilities • any other occupancy with an occupant load greater than 5000 • power-generating stations, water treatment for potable water, wastewater treatment facilities, and other public utility facilities not included in occupancy category IV • buildings and other structures not included in occupancy category IV containing sufficient quantities of toxic or explosive substances to be dangerous to the public if released
IV	buildings and other structures designed as essential facilities, including but not limited to • hospitals and other health care facilities having surgery or emergency treatment facilities • fire, rescue, and police stations and emergency vehicle garages • designated earthquake, hurricane, or other emergency shelters • designated emergency preparedness, communication, and operation centers and other facilities required for emergency response • power-generating stations and other public utility facilities required as emergency backup facilities for occupancy category IV structures • structures containing highly toxic materials as defined by Sec. 307 of the 2006 International Building Code where the quantity of the material exceeds the maximum allowable quantities of Table 307.1(2) • aviation control towers, air traffic control centers, and emergency aircraft hangars • buildings and other structures having critical national defense functions • water treatment facilities required to maintain water pressure for fire suppression

Table 8
Values of Site Coefficient F_a

site class	mapped spectral response acceleration at short period				
	$S_s \leq 0.25$	$S_s = 0.50$	$S_s = 0.75$	$S_s = 1.00$	$S_s \geq 1.25$
A	0.8	0.8	0.8	0.8	0.8
B	1.0	1.0	1.0	1.0	1.0
C	1.2	1.2	1.1	1.0	1.0
D	1.6	1.4	1.2	1.1	1.0
E	2.5	1.7	1.2	0.9	0.9

Adapted with permission from the 2006 International Building Code. Copyright 2006.
Washington, DC: International Code Council, Inc.

Table 9
Values of Site Coefficient F_v

site class	mapped spectral response acceleration at 1-second period				
	$S_1 \leq 0.1$	$S_1 = 0.2$	$S_1 = 0.3$	$S_1 = 0.4$	$S_1 \geq 0.5$
A	0.8	0.8	0.8	0.8	0.8
B	1.0	1.0	1.0	1.0	1.0
C	1.7	1.6	1.5	1.4	1.3
D	2.4	2.0	1.8	1.6	1.5
E	3.5	3.2	2.8	2.4	2.4

Adapted with permission from the 2006 International Building Code. Copyright 2006.
Washington, DC: International Code Council, Inc.

Table 10
Wall Pressure Coefficients

wall pressure coefficients, C_p			
surface	L/B	C_p	use with
windward wall	all values	0.8	q_z
leeward wall	0–1	−0.5	q_h
	2	−0.3	
	≥4	−0.2	
side wall	all values	−0.7	q_h

Adapted from the 2005 edition of the ASCE/SEI 7 standard, *Minimum Design Loads for Buildings and Other Structures*, with permission from the publisher, the American Society of Civil Engineers.

Table 11
Allowable Stress Design Selection

Allowable Stress Design Selection Table
For shapes used as beams S_x

$F_y = 50$ ksi			S_x	Shape	Depth d	F_y'	$F_y = 36$ ksi		
L_c	L_u	M_R					L_c	L_u	M_R
ft	ft	kip-ft	in³		in	ksi	ft	ft	kip-ft
6.7	**8.7**	**270**	**98.3**	**W 18 × 55**	**18¹⁄₈**	**–**	**7.9**	**12.1**	**195**
10.8	21.9	268	97.4	W 12 × 72	12¹⁄₄	52.3	12.7	30.5	193
5.6	**6.0**	**260**	**94.5**	**W 21 × 50**	**20⁷⁄₈**	**–**	**6.9**	**7.8**	**187**
6.4	10.3	254	92.2	W 16 × 57	16³⁄₈	–	7.5	14.3	183
9.0	15.5	254	92.2	W 14 × 61	13⁷⁄₈	–	10.6	21.5	183
6.7	**7.9**	**244**	**88.9**	**W 18 × 50**	**18**	**–**	**7.9**	**11.0**	**176**
10.7	20.0	238	87.9	W 12 × 65	12¹⁄₈	43.0	12.7	27.7	174
4.7	**5.9**	**224**	**81.6**	**W 21 × 44**	**20⁵⁄₈**	**–**	**6.6**	**7.0**	**162**
6.3	9.1	223	81.0	W 16 × 50	16¹⁄₄	–	7.5	12.7	160
5.4	6.5	217	78.8	W 18 × 46	18	–	6.4	9.4	156
9.0	17.5	215	78.0	W 12 × 58	12¹⁄₄	–	10.6	24.4	154
7.2	12.7	214	77.8	W 14 × 53	13⁷⁄₈	–	8.5	17.7	154
6.3	8.2	200	72.7	W 16 × 45	16¹⁄₈	–	7.4	11.4	144
9.0	15.9	194	70.6	W 12 × 53	12	55.9	10.6	22.0	140
7.2	11.5	193	70.3	W 14 × 48	13³⁄₄	–	8.5	16.0	139

Adapted from *Manual of Steel Construction (ASD)*, copyright © American Institute of Steel Construction, Inc.
Reprinted with permission. All rights reserved.

Table 12
Velocity Pressure Exposure Coefficients, K_h and K_z

height above ground level, z		exposure			
		B		C	D
(ft)	(m)	case 1	case 2	cases 1 & 2	cases 1 & 2
0–15	(0–4.6)	0.70	0.57	0.85	1.03
20	(6.1)	0.70	0.62	0.90	1.08
25	(7.6)	0.70	0.66	0.94	1.12
30	(9.1)	0.70	0.70	0.98	1.16
40	(12.2)	0.76	0.76	1.04	1.22
50	(15.2)	0.81	0.81	1.09	1.27
60	(18)	0.85	0.85	1.13	1.31
70	(21.3)	0.89	0.89	1.17	1.34
80	(24.4)	0.93	0.93	1.21	1.38
90	(27.4)	0.96	0.96	1.24	1.40
100	(30.5)	0.99	0.99	1.26	1.43

Adapted from the 2005 edition of the ASCE/SEI 7 standard, *Minimum Design Loads for Buildings and Other Structures*, with permission from the publisher, the American Society of Civil Engineers.

Table 13
Columns: W Shapes
Allowable Axial Loads (in kips)

designation		W14												
wt/ft		82		74		68		61		53		48		43	
F_y (ksi)		36	50	36	50	36	50	36	50	36	50	36	50	36	50
effective length (ft)	0	521	723	471	654	432	600	387	537	337	468	305	423	272	377
	6	482	657	436	595	400	545	358	487	302	408	273	369	244	329
	7	474	643	429	581	393	533	351	476	295	395	266	356	237	317
	8	465	627	421	567	385	519	345	464	286	380	258	343	230	305
	9	456	610	412	552	377	505	338	452	277	364	250	329	223	292
	10	446	593	403	536	369	491	330	439	268	348	242	313	215	279
	11	435	575	394	520	360	475	322	425	258	330	233	298	207	264
	12	425	555	384	502	351	459	314	410	248	312	224	281	199	249
	14	402	515	363	465	332	425	297	379	226	273	204	245	181	216
	16	377	471	341	426	311	388	278	346	202	229	182	206	161	181
	18	351	423	317	383	289	348	258	310	177	184	159	165	140	144
	20	323	372	292	337	266	305	237	272	149	149	133	133	117	117
	22	293	318	265	287	241	259	214	230	123	123	110	110	96	96
	24	261	267	236	241	214	218	190	193	104	104	93	93	81	81
	26	227	227	206	206	186	186	165	165	88	88	79	79	69	69
	28	196	196	177	177	160	160	142	142	76	76	68	68	60	60
	30	171	171	154	154	139	139	124	124	66	66	59	59	52	52
	31	160	160	145	145	131	131	116	116	62	52	56	56	49	49
	32	150	150	136	136	123	123	109	109	58	58				
	34	133	133	120	120	109	109	96	96						
	36	119	119	107	107	97	97	86	86						
	38	106	106	96	96	87	87	77	77						

Table 14
Bearing Bolt Values
Allowable Loads (in kips)

material thickness (in)	$F_u = 58$ ksi bolt diameter (in)			$F_u = 65$ ksi bolt diameter (in)			$F_u = 70$ ksi bolt diameter (in)			$F_u = 100$ ksi bolt diameter (in)		
	3/4	7/8	1	3/4	7/8	1	3/4	7/8	1	3/4	7/8	1
1/8	6.5	7.6	8.7	7.3	8.5	9.8	7.9	9.2	10.5	11.3	13.1	15.0
3/16	9.8	11.4	13.1	11.0	12.8	14.6	11.8	13.8	15.8	16.9	19.7	22.5
1/4	13.1	15.2	17.4	14.6	17.1	19.5	15.8	18.4	21.0	22.5	26.3	30.0
5/16	16.3	19.0	21.8	18.3	21.3	24.4	19.7	23.0	26.3	28.1	32.8	37.5
3/8	19.6	22.8	26.1	21.9	25.6	29.3	23.6	27.6	31.5	33.8	39.4	45.0
7/16	22.8	26.6	30.5	25.6	29.9	34.1	27.6	32.2	36.8		45.9	52.5
1/2	26.1	30.5	34.8	29.3	34.1	39.0	31.5	36.8	42.0			60.0
9/16	29.4	34.3	39.2	32.9	38.4	43.9		41.3	47.3			
5/8	32.6	38.1	43.5		42.7	48.8		45.9	52.5			
11/16		41.9	47.9		46.9	53.6			57.8			
3/4		45.7	52.2			58.5						
13/16			56.6									
7/8			60.9									
15/16												
1	52.2	60.9	69.6	58.5	68.3	78.0	63.0	73.5	84.0	90.0	105.0	120.0

Adapted from *Manual of Steel Construction (ASD)*, copyright © American Institute of Steel Construction, Inc. Reprinted with permission. All rights reserved.